NARRATIVE AS THEME

Narrative as Theme

.... Studies in French Fiction ....

.... By Gerald Prince ....

.... University of Nebraska Press ....

.... Lincoln : London ....

© 1992 by the
University of Nebraska Press
All rights reserved
Manufactured in the United
States of America
The paper in this book meets
the minimum
requirements of American National Standard for
Information Sciences – Permanence of Paper
for Printed Library Materials,
ANSI Z39.48–1984.

Library of Congress Cataloging in Publication Data
Prince, Gerald.
Narrative as theme: studies in French fiction / by
Gerald Prince.
p.cm. Includes bibliographical references and index.
ISBN 0-8032-3699-9 (alk. paper)
1. French fiction – History and criticism. 2. Narration (Rhetoric) in literature. I. Title.
PQ631.P7 1992 843.009′23-dc20 91-22481 CIP

Contents

Preface vii

1. On Theme and Theming 1
2. The Theme of Narrative 14
3. The Disnarrated 28
4. Singular Narrative 39
5. Candid Explanations 51
6. Written Narrative 65
7. Narrative as Antagonist 77
8. Nausea and Narrative 91
9. How to Redo Things with Words 104
10. Narrative All the Same 121

Notes 133

Bibliography 149

Index 159

Preface

Narrative has long been a thematic concern of narrative and has even been considered its privileged theme. Yet there is, to my knowledge, no book-length study of narrative as theme and, more specifically, no sustained inquiry into fictional views of the relation between narrative and truth (is the former adequate to the latter? can it be? under what conditions? with what results? and so on). This book constitutes an attempt to explore some of these views.

The first part is the more general and "theoretical" in nature. In Chapter 1, I review some of the basic dimensions and characteristics of theme and examine some of the (textual) factors and (conceptual) operations that enter into theming, into relating a given theme and a given text, into grasping the latter in terms of the former. Using *Eugénie Grandet* as an example, I insist on theming as a function of both text and themer. In Chapter 2, I discuss some of the manifestations of and reasons for the popularity of the theme of narrative in our time; I draw from them certain provisory lessons relevant to thematics and to narrative as theme; I sketch some possible contributions of thematics to poetics, hermeneutics, and the history of discourse; and I outline the structuration of the theme of narrative that constitutes my point of departure and guide in studying what narratives say about narrative. In Chapter 3, I define and describe the *disnarrated*, which comprises all those passages in a text that consider what did not or does not happen but could have happened. I argue that it acts as an instrument for reading the text's attitude toward narrative.

The second part of the book focuses on seven novels, devoting a chapter to each and, more particularly though not exclusively, to its estimation of the consonance of narrative and truth. *La Princesse de Clèves* implies that narrative can be adequate not only to common truths but also to exceptional ones, if it dares to be exceptional. *Candide* suggests that a narrative honoring facts, taking the singularities and discontinuities of existence into account, and rejecting spurious causality, teleology, and totalization succeeds in showing the way things are. *Madame Bovary* intimates that a "good" narrative, a narrative concordant to the world, must avoid the mercenary and the personal and must refuse the itineraries and imperatives of oral communication. According to *Bel-Ami*, narrative, in order to be true, must transcend narrative and its traditional characteristics. In *La Nausée*, narrative is always fictional and history is just a story, yet the best narrative may be not so much the one attempting to sever all ties with reality and to take refuge in pure fiction as the one self-consciously trying to organize the data of reality in order to give them a particular meaning and force. *La Route des Flandres* promotes a narrative without narrativity so as to approximate the specific situations and events it cannot entirely grasp or elucidate. Finally, though narrative in *Rue des Boutiques Obscures*, because of the problematic nature of life, fails to reconstruct what took place, narrative paradoxically proves successful through the very fact that it is told and thus (re)constitutes life.

To exploit and explore the theme of narrative, I have relied on the French literary tradition: it is the one I know best. I have tried to assemble a varied and representative corpus: classical, modern, and postmodern novels in the first and the third person, explicitly interested in narrative or seemingly uninterested in it, with significant psychological, philosophical, sociological, or formal concerns, and—most important for my purpose— exemplifying basic positions with regard to the truth-value of narrative.

In my analyses, I have been guided by two principles (without becoming their slave): sticking to the text, and basing my conclusions on the answers to a stable set of questions (who narrates, within the world presented? to whom? in what circumstances and why? what is disnarrated? what is narrative compared to or contrasted with? what, according to the text, is the veracity quotient and the value of the narratives recounted? what factors affect or determine this veracity and value? and, last, what (truth) value, if any, does the text attribute to narrative in general?).

Though I have chosen to follow chronological order, that choice was motivated by convenience rather than by any desire to suggest a historical account of the theme of narrative. Such an account could, of course, be derived from my presentation, and it would be familiar (going from a relatively unproblematic congruity of narrative and truth to an increasingly problematic relation between the two) but not necessarily accurate. After all, with regard to narrative as theme, Camus's *La Peste* is not very different from *Candide*, and the seventeenth-century anti-novel anticipates the twentieth-century New Novel.

Finally, in the hope of increasing the readability of my study, I have elected to substitute my own English translations for all quotations from French primary and secondary sources.

I think that the French texts cited are easily obtainable, and I believe that my translations are correct.

.....

I should like to thank the following journals for permission to use articles of mine that I have slightly revised for this study: *Poétique* (no.64, 1985) for "Thématiser"; *Communications* (no.47, 1988) for "Le Thème du récit"; *Style* (vol.22, 1988) for "The Disnarrated"; *Saggi e Ricerche di Letteratura Francese* (vol.22, 1983) for "Candid Explanations"; *French Forum* (vol.11, 1986) for "*Bel-Ami* and Narrative as Antagonist"; *MLN* (vol.103, 1988) for "How to Redo Things with Words: *La Route des Flandres.*"

I also thank the University of Pennsylvania for granting me a teaching leave in the spring of 1990, and Ellen F. Prince for invaluable technical advice.

1... On Theme and Theming

In *Form and Meaning in Fiction*, Norman Friedman writes: "*Theme* is one of those crucial but shifting terms in contemporary criticism which for the old-fashioned critic means message or moral, while for the New Critic it means total meaning or form. It can also refer variously to the basic problem, issue, or question embodied in the work (the relation of the individual to society, for example); any recurrence in the work, as in motif or leitmotif (the rain theme in *A Farewell to Arms*, for example); any pervasive element or factor (the theme of infection in *Bleak House*); any dominant subject matter or character type (the love theme, for example, or the woman theme); any aspect of the content (the theme of religion or travel); or, as in Northrop Frye, the 'meaning,' 'conceptual content,' 'idea,' or 'point' of the work."[1] This characterization of theme, given its looseness, is perhaps not reassuring, but I am afraid that it is pretty accurate. At least, the organizers of an international colloquium devoted to thematics and held several years after the publication of Friedman's book seemed to share his caution: "Are themes concepts (love, death, the city, the double . . .), aggregates of concepts (the prodigal son, the young woman and death . . .), or else judgments (life is a dream, there is no happy love)?"[2]

So does the library catalogue at the University of Pennsylvania where, under "theme," I found a motley collection of titles, referring to the theme of the flea and that of the tree, the theme of Faust and of Don Juan, the theme of pregnancy and the theme of eating, the theme of death, rebellion, and redemption. A search through critico-theoretical, philosophic, linguistic, and Artificial Intelligence–oriented material yielded suggestive but not much more consistent or firmer results: theme is both intra- and extratextual, immanent and transcendent, what the work speaks about and what allows one to speak about the work; theme is to plot as meaning is to form; theme is that which plot constitutes a temporal projection of; theme is what is made of a topic; theme is a main idea in a text, a central thread, a minimum generalization; theme is a highly abstract semantic category subsuming a set of motifs or minimal and concrete thematic units; theme is a frame, a macrostructure, a reality model, a system organizing knowledge about some phenomenon in the world; theme is what a text or part thereof is about; theme is a general thought unifying and summarizing a series of sentences; theme is a proposition entailed by a discourse sequence.[3] Even Teun van Dijk's more formal characterization of that last definition—"a proposition T is a topic [or theme[4]] of a sequence of propositions $\Sigma = \triangleleft p_1, p_2, \ldots, p_n \triangleright$ iff for each $p_i \in \Sigma$ there is a subsequence Σ_k of Σ such that $p_i \in \Sigma_k$, and for each successive Σ_k there is a p_j such that $\Sigma_k \Rightarrow p_j$ and $T \Rightarrow p_j$"[5]—even so formal a characterization does not, as van Dijk himself recognizes and quite apart from the question of its adequacy, make explicit all the intuitive notions he uses in trying to clarify the concept theme.[6] No provision is made for recursiveness, no guarantee is supplied that the sequences are ordered, and no strict definition is given of the notion of entailment for sequences of propositions.

Rather than attempt to arrive at a definition of theme that

would be more rigorous but might not be more adequate, I focus here on the "what" designated by at least some of the characterizations I mentioned as well as on some of my own intuitive formulations about theme. I try to restate and unfold that "what" (at times by proceeding negatively and by distinguishing it from such commonly related notions as topic, motif, or plot). I sketch some of the elements entering into theming, into (re)organizing and grasping a text in terms of theme, into reading it for or according to theme. And I give a quick example of the theming of a text with one theme.

.....

One point seems relatively clear: theme expresses a relation of being about. To say that the theme of a story S is T usually means at the very least that S is about T (about the individual in relation to society, about the rain, about love, about religion, about the dreamlike nature of life, about Faust, or Don Juan, or eating, or pregnancy). Now, this aboutness is not a semantic aboutness (as defined by Nelson Goodman, say, or Hilary Putnam).[7] Given the text "All crows are black," in the context "All crows are birds," the text is semantically about not only the class of crows but also the class of black things, the class of things that are not black, and the class of things that are not crows. Yet I would not want to say that one of the themes (or, for that matter, topics or subjects) of that text is non-black things or non-crows. Rather, I might say that one of its themes (or topics, or subjects) is crows (or, possibly, birds). In other words, I would rely on a notion of pragmatic aboutness (as developed by P. F. Strawson or Tanya Reinhart)[8] whereby a text can be pragmatically about (that which is meant by) those units explicitly constituting it, or those classes of which they are members, or those categories which they illustrate. More specifically, a text is pragmatically about those elements of it (or the sets, aggregates, and concepts they constitute or specify) that make it relevant in a given context.[9]

Another point seems relatively clear: though there are many things that a text can be said to be pragmatically about, not all of them are equivalent to themes. "Un Coeur simple," for instance, is about Félicité, yet I do not believe that the heroine constitutes one of the themes of Flaubert's short story. Similarly, "New Jersey is flat along the east and southern portion; the northwestern region is mountainous; the coastal climate is mild, but there is considerable cold in the mountain areas during the winter months" is certainly about New Jersey; however, once again, I would not say that New Jersey represents one of its themes. To take another kind of example, Charles Perrault's "Le Petit Chaperon rouge" is about a little girl who ends up eaten by a wolf, and the parable of the Good Samaritan is about a man who helps another man lying half dead in the road; but these characterizations function as plot summaries rather than thematic statements. There are also many terms related to the term "theme"—motif, topos, topic or subject,[10] symbol—and sometimes confused with it. I believe that the following distinctions may be helpful. A motif is not a theme but a possible illustration of one; or, to put it differently and more precisely, a motif is a member of the set of objects characterizing a theme extensionally; relative to a given semantic domain, if motif M represents theme T, T cannot represent M. A topos—the wise fool, the aged child, the *locus amoenus*—is also not a theme but a stable configuration of motifs. A topic is either the most prominent element in a text, the element associated with the most numerous or salient predicates, or else a class or aggregate of which this most prominent textual element is a member or constituent. Finally, a symbol, as opposed to a theme, is what it is as well as what it represents (it is the very conjunction of a motif and the theme concretized by that motif).

Perhaps the notion "theme" can be further specified as follows. One of the differences between, say, a plot, a topic, and a theme results from the kinds of referents they (can) pertain to. Whereas a plot is linked to (particular) events, for instance, and whereas a topic can be equivalent to (a set of) specific and concrete entities (Félicité, New Jersey), a theme involves only general and abstract entities: ideas, thoughts, beliefs, and so on. When I speak of the theme of rain, the theme of Antigone, or the theme of Creon, I merely use a kind of shorthand to evoke certain philosophical, ideological, or moral views or concepts: the possibility of cleansing and redemption, the primacy of the individual, the exigencies of the social order. In other words, if theme is a macrostructural category or frame allowing for the unification of distinct (and discontinuous) textual elements, it is an "idea" frame rather than an action frame (plot), an existent frame (character, setting), or an image frame (imagery). Moreover, theme is distinctive, if not unique, because of its relation to textual surface structure: it does not *consist of* textual units, and it is different from them in kind; rather, theme is *illustrated by* any number of textual units (or by other macrostructural categories, such as plot, or by other themes), just as a general law or rule or precept is illustrated by an example. Saying that a textual unit U illustrates a theme T is not equivalent to saying that U is a member of the class of Ts or that U is part of the aggregate T; instead, it is equivalent to saying that U suitably resembles a paradigm case of T.

.....

If theme expresses a pragmatic relation of being about, if it pertains to general and abstract rather than specific and concrete entities, and if it is illustrated and not constituted by the text or its components, theming consists in relating a set of textual units and a theme T through such predicates as "illustrates T," "is representative of T," "is an example of T," "suitably resembles a paradigm case of T." In other words, in transforming textual elements into thematic ones, the themer ultimately supplies (assumes some responsibility for) not only the predicate but also the theme. The selection of the latter describes one of two main trajectories (or their combination): (1) some general abstract truth or belief is related—through analogy, synecdoche, metonymy—to some set of textual elements that are taken to illustrate it; (2) some set of textual elements implies or suggests a general proposition, and this proposition is taken to constitute a theme.

Several rather loose constraints apply to these theming trajectories. First, a theme is seldom if ever retained as pertinent to a text or subtext if it turns out to be exemplified by very few textual elements. If an entire novel contained only one (possible) illustration of death, for instance, we would not—or, rather, we might but I do not think that most of us would— take the theme of death to be relevant to it. To use a more concrete example, we would not say that one of the themes of the parable of the Good Samaritan is death, even though the parable discusses the treatment that a man lying half dead in the road gets from his fellow men. Second, a theme is seldom relied upon to organize and grasp some less prominent (backgrounded) elements in a text unless it is also used to organize and grasp some more prominent (foregrounded) elements. Given "It was six o'clock, and the argument between John and his father was growing progressively more heated. At seven o'clock, the father decided that he had better leave the house," we would probably not rely on a theme such as "the passage of time" to unify the temporal notations (another kind of frame—a setting frame, say—might, of course, be invoked). Third, given a set of textual elements that can be thought to illustrate two different themes, one of which can also be thought to exemplify the other, we would tend to retain the former rather than the latter because the theming would perforce require fewer operations and would also capture more of the specificity of the set involved. In other words, the thematic frame (ultimately) selected would be the smaller one; the generalization adopted, the more modest one. Though both the theme of emotion and the theme of fear, for instance, could frame a passage depicting a character's painful agitation in the presence of some threat, fear rather than emotion would be taken to be the theme of the passage. Fourth and finally, of two themes, one that unifies a certain set of textual elements and another that unifies a proper subset of that set, the first would ultimately be retained. This may explain why certain themes—the nature-and-culture dichotomy, the disparity between sign and object, the power of divine redemption and retribution, sexuality, narrative—are privileged over others: at different times and in different places, they are considered powerful enough to allow for the coordination of indefinitely large numbers of textual or thematic elements.

.....

A rapid sketch of the theming of a particular text in terms of one theme will clarify my views further. I want to stress that my goal is not to describe the actual process of theming. In the first place, as must have been obvious, I do not believe that hard and fast rules apply. Besides, mine is not exactly an empirical study. I take theming a text and a theming of a text to be distinct, though related, and I focus on the latter. In presenting my account, I often refer to *Eugénie Grandet*.[11] I do not intend to give a detailed reading of that text, but I hope that my references will help to elucidate theme and theming and to show why it is that we frequently propose acceptable though different and sometimes incompatible thematic interpretations of the same work.

In order to read a particular text in terms of one theme, we assign thematic status to constituent units of that text according to a number of (idiosyncratic and cultural) codes or subcodes: we label them as illustrative of a certain theme. The nature and size of the units—like the nature and size of the codes—may vary from one themer to another and, for the same themer, from one point of the text to another: the unit could consist of a single word, a phrase, a sentence, a group of sentences, any one of their features or interrelations, and so on. Of course, not all the units making up the text would necessarily be retained. Given *Eugénie Grandet*, I might, for example and to begin with, eliminate from consideration units in the work that make it inconsistent: was Nanon hired by Grandet in 1791 or much earlier (30, 31)? does Guillaume Grandet owe two million francs or four (111)? is Eugénie twenty-two or twenty-three in December 1819 (36, 196)? does Charles send her a check for 8,000 or 8,100 francs (242, 247)? Depending on the theme adopted, I might also regard as irrelevant to my purpose some of the lines describing the detail of Grandet's financial operations ("His two thousand acres of forest land had brought him six hundred thousand francs .... The 20 percent he could earn quickly on the returns, which were at 70 francs, tempted him," 117), and I might ignore some of the passages depicting various aspects of his clothing ("he wore ... a large brown suit with big flaps, a black tie, and a Quaker hat. His gloves . . . lasted him twenty months and, to keep them clean, he put them on the edge of his hat, always in the same place, with a methodical gesture," 20). In other words, the textual illustration of my elected theme is not necessarily identical to the text of the novel.

But how is the thematic relevance or irrelevance of a unit determined? As a themer, I select or construct a thematic frame (subsuming an indefinite number of other frames) in terms of which a large number of units (the larger the better!) can be made to blend together. This frame is (based on) a model deriving from an intra- or extratextual reality and its selection and constitution are conditioned by my knowledge, interests, and goals. I might decide, for instance, that in *Eugénie Grandet* I am faced above all with a depiction of ambiguous sexuality and its vicissitudes: as her last name suggests, Eugénie is big and strong, with "none of the cuteness that the common folk admire" (83); she has "an enormous head, the masculine yet delicate brow of the Jupiter of Phidias" (82); she reminds people not so much of her mother as of her father, whose vocabulary, mannerisms, and voice she comes to adopt; she longs for Charles because he is so pretty and coquettish and "curly-haired like a girl" (185); and the very sight of him provokes "in her heart those emotions of exquisite pleasure that the fantastic figures of women drawn by Westall . . . and engraved by Finden . . . provoke in a young man"(56). Or I might see the novel as an illustration of *l'argent ne fait pas le bonheur* (money doesn't make happiness); I might consider it to provide a fine example of the exploitation of human beings by other human beings; I might take it to be a specification of the gap between sign and object. Any unit that would not evoke the frame, and could be related to it only at the cost of an extensive series of operations,

I might judge irrelevant. Similarly, any unit that could not be made to cohere easily with other units, whether by metonymic, synecdochic, or analogical relations (one unit prolongs another, is causally related to it, or is in "natural" proximity with it; one unit specifies, includes, or generalizes another; one unit contrasts with or parallels another), would also be irrelevant.

Note that although certain units in a given work are eliminated from consideration, the textual basis of my theme is by no means a subset of that work: if I reduce the work in order to interpret it, and if I reduce it as I interpret it (any framing context having to result in the suppression of at least some of the potential meanings of textual constituents), I also expand it. In the first place, relating units to a frame and blending them with other units entails or allows for (1) the specification of what the work does not make explicit (through filling the "gaps" between the units involved or making contextual associations and connotations apparent); (2) the derivation of non-trivial pragmatic implications from the union of any two (sets of) units;[12] and (3) the addition of evaluative commentary indicating the status of the units in relation to one another and to the frame. Moreover, and just as important, the frame selected or constructed may itself subsume a certain number of constituents, and these may combine with the units retained to yield further pragmatic implications. Should the exploitation theme, for example, involve a certain number of Marxist constructs (should I theme *Eugénie Grandet* in Marxist terms), "Marx" or some of it becomes part of my material; and should the sexuality theme involve a certain number of Freudian categories (should I theme *Eugénie Grandet* in Freudian terms), "Freud" becomes part of my material. Of course, I might also theme the novel in terms of "common sense" (whatever that is), or I might theme it in terms of my idiosyncrasies and momentary preoccupations. But in any case, and to put it bluntly, the text (to be) themed always includes the context of the themer. To put it even more bluntly, I always make the work I theme.

Suppose I select or construct a frame whereby *Eugénie Grandet* is an illustration of the gap between sign and object. I might do it not only because of my inclinations (I happen to like reading every text in terms of this gap) but also because of the many encouragements I find in Balzac's text. After all, the very first feeling described by the text, in the very first sentence, gives rise to an interpretive remark: "One finds in certain provincial cities houses the sight of which inspires a melancholy equal to that provoked by the darkest cloisters, the dullest *landes*, or the saddest ruins. Perhaps there is at once in these houses the silence of the cloister and the aridity of the *landes* and the dead bones of ruins" (5). The addresses to the narratee underline the importance of experience for proper deciphering: for example, "Few people know the importance of a *salle* in the small towns of Anjou, Touraine, and Berry. The *salle* is, at the same time, the antechamber, the living-room, the study, the boudoir, the dining-room" (27); or else, "He who has known the most powerful of passions, one whose duration is each day abridged by age, by time, by a mortal illness, by some human disaster, he will understand Eugénie's torments" (176). The narrator's many hesitations (*peut-être, peut-être, peut-être*), like the numerous metalinguistic passages ("Here perhaps it is appropriate to note that, in Touraine, in Anjou, in Poitou, in Brittany, the word *bonhomme* is bestowed upon the most cruel as well as the most easygoing men, as soon as they reach a certain age," 124), bring out the difficulty of going beyond the sign to the thing itself. And at least one long piece of commentary is explicitly devoted to the role of the interpreter in the act of interpretation: when Eugénie reads Charles's letter to Annette, she finds in it what she herself has put in: "For young women who get a religious upbringing and who are innocent and pure, everything is love as soon as they step in the enchanted regions of love. They walk surrounded by the celestial light that their soul projects and that falls like rays on their lover; they color him with the fires of their own feeling and lend him their most beautiful thoughts" (152).

Similarly, references to the theater as well as to the difference between appearance and reality abound in the novel; signs, in the world depicted, are said to be modified and even destroyed by the passage of time (e.g., 6, 7, 26); names are shown to be arbitrary (with Judge Cruchot becoming Cruchot de Bonfons, C. de Bonfons, then M. de Bonfons; and with Charles becoming Carl Sepherd, then comte d'Aubrion); oral (and, even more so, written) language institutes a distance that only the heart can perhaps transcend; and money, the sign par excellence, the ultimate *valant-pour*, often occupies center stage. Suppose I selected the sign-and-object frame. I would then select all those units possibly referring, alluding, or connected to the relation between sign and object (and their extra- or intratextual connotations), and to capture the specificity of Balzac's illustration I would further organize them in terms of a set of oppositions subsumed by the sign-object opposition: miserliness and love, movement ("it comes, it goes, it sweats, it produces," 195) and immobility, action and passivity, the mind and the heart, the relative and the absolute. Through summary and paraphrase I might arrive at an account of Balzac's novel in which the heroine, after long and brutal years that leave her essentially unchanged, concludes that objects as such are unattainable in her world and seeks refuge in "the proud love that lives on its pain and dies of it" (243), love-in-itself, love intransitive.

.....

Theming a text, as I hope I have made clear, thus depends not only on the "text itself" but also on the themer, the frame adopted, the units selected, and the operations executed to make them cohere and yield additional meaning, not to mention the summaries and paraphrases performed. If there is any difference between theming and good theming, the latter might be said to obtain when the frame adopted is considered adequate to the text: when it accounts for an appropriate number of acceptable units in terms of an appropriate number of valid operations. Fortunately, or unfortunately, what is appropriate, valid, or acceptable varies considerably from one set of themers to another. Another difference probably worthy of comment is the one between theming a literary or a narrative text and theming another kind of text. The former might restrict itself to themes pertaining to the production, nature, and reception of literature or narrative—reading, writing, telling, and representing, and so on—and it might give rise to the kind of *thématique restreinte* that Naomi Schor, among others, called for.[13] But though there may be affinities between literary or narrative texts and certain themes, especially under certain historical conditions, I do not believe that any theme is, by definition, always favored (or resisted) by literature or narrative. Perhaps some motifs and topoi constitute categories that are distinctive of some forms of art (though I tend to doubt it), but themes, like topics and symbols, do not. In short, thematics is not only or not so much a subset of artistic, literary, or narrative studies as it is part of the study of culture, interpretation, and cognition.

2... The Theme of Narrative

Studying the discourse of secondary discourses, Michel Charles underlines the panlinguisticism, the pantextualism of our era and writes the following about the literary text: "Since there are cases, which are neither rare nor linked to any modernity whatsoever, in which the literary text examines itself, it is then comparable, from the point of view that interests us here, to a secondary discourse. Better: one can show this without excessive difficulty. After all, since the modern critic has an extremely rich, refined, and varied metaphorics, there are hardly any sheets, edges, folds, rules, hardly any movements, lines, deployments that cannot refer to writing, to the pen, to the page. If we add erasers, ink, machines, the whole little factory of the potterer who was once called a scriptor, then we can have a sufficient number of landing sites to make elaborate reading processes reach the most diverse metaphoric fields. This is so true that among the great hermeneutic systems of our time—ideological interpretation, libidinal interpretation—one should probably mention scriptural interpretation. And it has to be said that modern poetics has played a not insignificant role in the contemporary renewal of this type of interpretation: one goes so easily from the autotelic nature of the message to the notion of its autoreferentiality."[1]

One could prolong these remarks by noting that autoreferentiality leads easily to autothematizing (the theme of the message is then the message itself) and by adding to the list of the great contemporary hermeneutic systems narrative interpretation. Indeed, the resort to narrative as theme and as the privileged theme of narrative has been remarkably frequent for more than twenty years (since the flowering of narratology, since the dazzling advances of dialogism and intertextuality). I would therefore like to mention some of the most eloquent manifestations of this popularity and to derive from them certain provisional lessons pertaining to thematics in general and the thematics of narrative in particular.

To be exploited and explored, the theme of narrative clearly did not have to wait for the theorists, critics, or novelists of the past two or three decades. Narrative has been around for a long time, perhaps forever; it has been known and recognized for a long time. If, as Claude Bremond emphasized, the discovery of themes parallels that of the world; if, to speak like Roland Barthes, everything that is noted is notable and therefore thematizable, it is normal that narrative, for a long time, has been the kernel of more or less explicit thematizations. Examples are as numerous in literature (in the exalted sense of the term) as they are in verbal art (in the broad sense). Before the great period of structuralism (and poststructuralism), there is, on the one hand, Maurice Blanchot, *Le Livre à venir*, narrative as the very event it constitutes; there is Jean-Paul Sartre's *La Nausée*, that tombstone of naturalism, which seems to ratify the divorce of living and telling; there is Louis-Ferdinand Céline and *Voyage au bout de la nuit*, Ramon Fernandez who makes of the *récit*— of "real" narrative—a genre contrary to the novel and inferior to it, Walter Benjamin and the problem of narrative authorities; there is surrealism, naturalism, and realism; there is, of course,

Tristram Shandy but also La Fontaine ("Le Lion et le chasseur," "La Jeune Veuve," "Le Pouvoir des fables"), Beroalde de Verville, and so on and so forth. On the other hand, in *The Types of the Folktale* by Antti Aarne and Stith Thompson as well as in their *Motif-Index of Folk Literature*, numerous examples of narrative as theme or motif are duly recorded: motif of the robber exposed by a story, motif of the storyteller interrupted, narrative as a means of survival, narrative and the preservation of law and order, narrative as an instrument of recognition, narrative as deception, and very many others.[2]

Still, it is from the 1960s on that the very word "narrative" begins to dislodge other terms: one will say "narrative" instead of "explanation" or "argumentation"; one will prefer "narrative" to "theory" or "hypothesis"; one will speak of "narrative" rather than "ideology"; one will substitute "narrative" for "fiction," "art," "message." Similarly, the notion of narrative is repeatedly called upon to characterize a multitude of intellectual enterprises and scientific fields: history, of course, but also philosophy, anthropology, and the natural sciences. The theme of narrative—the thematic frame "narrative"—is intensively (if often implicitly and perhaps unconsciously) utilized and gives rise to "narrative" readings of texts that have already been interpreted (too) many times; I mobilized it myself to study such different works as *Le Moyen de parvenir* and *Le Nœud de vipères*.[3] It becomes, in fact, the preferred theme of any great narrative, the theme indispensable to any narrative: I read in Jean Ricardou that "great narratives are recognizable by the sign that the fiction they propose is nothing other than the dramatization of their own functioning"; in Tzvetan Todorov that narrative constitutes the essential theme of *La Queste del Saint Graal,* just as it constitutes the essential theme of "all narrative, but always in a different way"; in Barthes that, in exemplary narratives, narration "is the (economic) theory of narration" and that ultimately there is no object of narrative—"the narrative concerns only itself: *the narrative tells itself.*"[4]

The issue (at least, the first one) is not to determine the justness of these affirmations. If it seems difficult to maintain that any narrative (any representation of one or more events, "Mary closed the window" as well as *War and Peace*) takes narrative as a theme, it is not easy to prove the contrary. I prefer to discuss very quickly what allows these affirmations, what partly institutes their possibility and their force, restricting myself—as much as possible and for the time being—to the domain of narrative texts, criticism, and theory.

One can assign at least three sets of reasons to the extraordinary success of narrative as thematic frame. I have already mentioned the slope going from autotelism to autoreferentiality and then to autothematizing. The work of art carries within itself and constitutes its own end: what would be more normal for it than to designate itself, to put its own nature in relief, to consider itself as a favored subject? Besides, language in general—indeed, every communicative and signifying practice—is partly defined in terms of a poetic, self-referential function. Language is not pure transparence. It does not merely describe the world; it makes it. It describes itself and the world it makes. The realist novel, which claims to avoid any self-examination the better to reach reality, represents not the apex to which an entire tradition led from its very birth on but—quite to the contrary—an aberration, a monstrosity. Doesn't the first novel, *Don Quijote*, offer a long meditation on itself in order to overcome the paradox of the feigned and the true? and isn't automeditation the only way, for any novelistic expression, to escape both naiveté and bad faith?[5] In his first narrative, says Jean-Pierre Faye, the first narrator ever to have a name may speak mostly of the wrath of Achilles, but in his second narrative he speaks above all of narrative. In fact, the more one thinks about it and in spite of all its claims, what is realism if not a reflexion on the consonances and dissonances between life and its narrative? and what is the greatest realist novel, perhaps, if not a new *Don Quijote*?[6]

Still, to gain approval, it is not enough (it was not enough!) merely to assert that such and such a narrative, like all narratives, discusses narrative. Such an assertion has to be supported on the basis of textual clues that generations of critics and readers who were, no doubt, perspicacious seem not to have noticed. If the modern discoverer or inventor of themes, the modern themer or thematizer should take risks, she or he should also keep the text in mind. And she or he does. Barthes, after all, is not content simply to declare that narrative in *Sarrasine* is presented as a contractual object and a merchandise; he traces how, in Balzac's novella, after some intensive bargaining, the narrator's narrative and the information it provides are (to be) exchanged for a body. Todorov shows how *The Odyssey* thematizes its genesis and transmission; how, in *A Thousand and One Nights*, to narrate well gives life and to be incapable of it leads to death; and how *La Queste del Saint Graal* is equivalent to a quest for narrative. More recently, Peter Brooks has argued forcefully that Julien Sorel, in wanting to invent his own plot, places himself in the domain of what is scandalous and to be condemned: that is to say, in the domain of the narratable.[7] Here lies, I think, the contribution of structuralism and, more particularly, of narratology and the reflection on narrative it deepens and fosters. By characterizing the elements integral to narrative; by determining the principles that govern its production; by studying the ways in which it can reflect itself, the techniques of *mise en abyme* of the code, the enunciation, and the enunciated; by specifying that there is in a narrative text a separable layer, a system constituting that which, in the text, makes up narrative proper, a configuration instituting the events as such, setting their beginning and their end, and dictating the itinerary which links them, narratology facilitates the choice of narrative as thematic frame. By (re)discovering and (re)inventing narrative, it allows one better to discover and better to invent the theme of narrative. A narrative consists of a certain number of narrative sequences, of minimal narratives linked through simple conjunction, embedding, or alternation; it involves a narrator and a narratee, a narrating and a narrated; it implies a relatively ordered series of transformations; it is both product and production, structure and structuration, object and act; it installs itself in repetition, moves in the desire for an end and for its deferral, deciphers memory and temporality: these are so many entries and reference points in the field of narrative as theme.

My third set of reasons comprises the notions of theme, thematic field, theming or thematization, and the extraordinary flexibility of their nature and use. As I have already mentioned, a theme is not composed of textual elements. It is illustrated by them. Indeed, a theme can be formulated independently from a given text: we speak of the theme of death, of the theme of rebellion, of forgiveness, of narrative. All at once *out of* the text (produced in other places, it is what allows us to give the text a certain coherence, to assign it a meaning, to relate it to a tradition) and *in* the text (it is what calls for and authorizes a certain interpretation), all at once exterior and interior, transcendent and immanent, it can of course be made explicit in a text; it can be given as such, expressed as such by the text. But most of the time it is a signified that is derived, in a more or less roundabout way, from a more or less homogeneous set of textual components and configurations, a meaning indirectly represented in, by, or through their world. I will add that in a given text the most explicit theme is not necessarily the most important one; that in any case its force for the themer does not always prove to be constraining; and that prominence is sometimes a function of secrecy or even absence.

As I have also mentioned earlier, and as I have just suggested again, the nature and the size of the textual elements transformed into thematic elements vary considerably from one text to the other, from one theme to the other, for the same theme in the same text. Any syntagm whatever—a word, a clause, a chapter, or any one of their traits and combinations—can represent the same theme. With regard to the thematic charge of formal or structural aspects, Thomas Pavel was able to show several years ago that the very course of a narrative, the deployment of its plot, is thematizable.[8] Pavel primarily educed the theme of temporality; but to say temporality is almost to say narrative, and besides, one could sketch a set of correspondences or connections between certain narrative types (as defined by their dynamics) and the theme of narrative: thus, Aarne and Thompson's "unfinished tales" could be linked to the theme of narrative as trap, their "endless tales" to that of narrative as adjournment, and so on. Similarly, as Philippe Hamon pointed out, nothing prevents us from thematizing phonetic components.[9] In fact, Ferdinand de Saussure's anagrams and Julia Kristeva's paragrams are here to suggest the thematic benefits of analyzing phonemes or graphemes, phones or letters. As for the number of textual elements mobilized by themings, it too varies considerably. After all, a theming can function more or less locally; it involves reductions and amplifications of the relevant text; and it can even develop in terms of an "unsaid" (this would yield, for example, the theme of the impossible or the absent narrative).

Furthermore, the strategies and operations used in a thematic exercise are remarkably supple, whether one chooses the text as a starting point and the theme as an endpoint or vice versa, whether one proceeds mainly through reduction or through expansion, whether one views the theme as a kind of frame allowing for a reading, for an interpretation, or whether on the contrary—and like Alexander Zholkovsky, for instance—one considers it to be a kernel of textual meaning that is intuitively graspable and that is incarnated, elaborated, carefully wrought out by the text. Zholkovsky's stance seems to me revealing in this regard precisely because it is one of the most rigorous stances in the field of thematics.[10] The fundamental operations thanks to which, according to him, a text is generated from a theme will allow me, I think, to indicate how easy it can be to exploit the theme of narrative. Thus, *concretization* establishes a link between the general and the particular (Man/carpenter, Mineral/pebble, City/Paris); it follows that the textual mention of any narrative or any narrative form whatever—fable, parable, novella, epic—can function as a sign of narrative as theme. *Division* connects an entity (an object, an event, a situation) and its components; one can therefore circulate between narrative and narrator or narratee, narrative and narrating or narrated, narrative and text, fiction, artifice, and so forth. *Repetition* sets an equivalence between a given entity and a given series of entities that are similar to it; now—I am quoting Marc Angenot—"there is hardly any novel which does not involve one or several narratives collected by the characters and, in turn, examined by the reader with regard to the role they play in the main plot."[11] Besides, and more generally, any narrative is made up of little narratives. When we add to these three moves the other operations isolated by Zholkovsky[12] and perhaps others still (narrative is memory/desire/repetition/ mirroring; now this text insists on memory, on desire; therefore it insists on narrative); when we consider too that all these operations can be applied and combined an indefinite number of times and that their mode of application and combination is not ordered, we see that one can discern a theme in what is most athematic and that the theme discerned may well be that of narrative.

Of course, all thematic analyses are not equally valuable; at any rate, they do not all meet with the same success, do not all get the same degree of approval. The theme discovered by a reading or employed for an interpretation must be adequate to the text; it must account for an appropriate number of acceptable textual units in terms of valid operations. But as I have already noted, what is appropriate, valid, or acceptable varies considerably with the context; besides, at least in the field of literary studies, criteria of effectiveness, of adequacy, of rigor find themselves balanced by criteria of ingeniousness and novelty. It therefore seems to me evident that thematics should resist the legislative temptation and should not exhaust itself in producing instruments to evaluate the well-foundedness of a theming or the beauty of a development based on this theme or that one. It seems to me even more evident that thematics cannot predict the textual manifestations of a theme, that it cannot specify its intension or extension. I note, in this regard, that the study of a theme (as distinct from the study of theme) is usually articulated in terms of a circumscribed corpus (the theme of the double *in* Dostoevsky, the theme of language *in* "Un Coeur simple," the theme of Prometheus *in* European literature) — and perhaps I should have entitled my own chapter "*Remarks* on the Theme of Narrative." There is no algorithm underlying the mutations of a theme, and if we want a thematics conforming to the nature of themes and to their potential, we must, like Roland Barthes, conceive it as infinite.[13]

These reflections do not necessarily imply that thematics is a discipline rebellious to any discipline, constituted by a set of lax and disparate practices, and attempting in one way or another (that is to say, in any and every way) to link texts and meanings. On the contrary, I am persuaded that thematics — as the "science" of theme and themes — has a role to play in the ongoing elaboration of a history of discourse, a hermeneutics, and a poetics. In at least three domains — pertaining to the topobiological, the cognitive, and the structural — considerable work remains to be done which would prolong the considerable work already done by thematicians and scholars of every persuasion.

In the first place — here I almost come back to my starting point, and I quickly note that the transparency and classification of texts in terms of certain themes are not irrelevant to the question — thematics can study the link between the elaborations or fortunes of a theme and the sociohistorical world(s) in which that theme appears and develops. Themes are born, they die, they are reborn, they have ups and downs; and their vitality is not only or not so much a function of their nature, their richness, their suppleness as it is a function of their situation. As far as the popularity of the theme of narrative is concerned, I think, for example, that apart from or along with the few arguments I have already retraced, one should take into account realism and its consequences (narrative as antagonist, as that which has to be avoided or neutralized); the commodification of literature and its decline as an instrument of knowledge (whence the increasing importance, for the literary work, of self-designation and self-justification); the death of God and then that of Man; the putting into question of origins, ends, and subjects (with the consequent collapse of *grands récits*, the preference for stories rather than theories or demonstrations, and the construction of hesitant and disabused narratives); and the postmodernist conviction, asserting itself in many domains, that for any work it is never a matter of illuminating nature but of exploring what is always already culture (in that case, narrative only reworks narrative).

Furthermore, one should attempt to describe as exactly, thoroughly, and economically as possible the operations and factors that allow or encourage the relating of a theme and a text. If studies such as Zholkovsky's show the way, the ten operations that he isolates do not quite avoid redundancy (*variation* is equivalent to the sum of several different concretizations); they do not quite escape heterogeneity or vagueness (I am thinking of *preparation*, which allows for the replacement of a given entity by a series of "inadequate" versions of it, ending with the entity itself); and—as suggested earlier—they do not quite include all the procedures mobilized by theming (the false syllogism, the simple antithesis, and so on: one should probably take into consideration every single tropical move!). Similarly, if many analysts have examined the factors determining thematic relief, they have been able to provide only a very general account of them: for example, contrasting explicit and implicit, direct and indirect, foregrounded and backgrounded, repeated and singular. A more detailed and more complete description of the means of circulation between theme and text would lead not only to a better understanding of what governs textual expansion and summary, textual memorization and interpretation, but also to a better estimate of the thematic transparency of texts (in terms of a given theme and lexicon), a transparency based on the number of operations necessary for the imposition or exposition of the theme, on the diversity of these operations, on their complexity and that of their mobilization. From the point of view that interests me here, isn't Sartre's *La Nausée*, in which several pages are explicitly devoted to the very nature and role of narrative, more transparent than Kafka's *The Castle*, where one would have to go, say, from the *arrivisme* of the protagonist to that of the novelist and therefore of the narrator in order to carry out a theming in terms of narrative?

Finally, though it is true that we cannot specify the intension or the extension of a theme, that we can neither circumscribe nor describe the domain it covers (like that of the world, this domain is infinitely renewable); though it is true that a theme constitutes a starting point or an endpoint for an indefinite number of itineraries and that we can neither enumerate all its subthemes and motifs or—*a fortiori*—characterize the structure they compose, the syntax that governs them, the play of similarities and oppositions that presides over their (re) grouping, this still does not prevent us from proposing one or several partial and temporary structurations of themes, one or several complexes of reference points which would partly organize their potential. This could lead not only to new thematizations but also to new classifications of texts according to their use of a given theme. Consider, for example, *A Thousand and*

One Nights, "La Jeune Veuve," and *La Peste*, of which it can be said that they all take narrative as a theme: in the first case it would roughly be a matter of narrating as an instrument of survival and, in the other two, a matter of the narrated as a source of truth.

In conclusion, I would like to sketch one such possible structuration of the theme of narrative. What the expression "theme of narrative" merely translates stenographically, what it abbreviates, is — to begin with — a double statement, two propositions: on the one hand, "narrative is an act"; on the other, "narrative is an object" (perhaps it should go without saying that many texts develop both propositions but that many insist on one at the expense of the other). This act and this object have a certain value (what they are or could be exchanged for, what they represent or could represent: a night of love in *Sarrasine*, redemption in *Le Nœud de vipères*, the truth in "La Jeune Veuve"), a value that is often underlined by an entity or process of which they constitute the contradictory, the contrary, the intensification, or the diminution (metaphysics in *Candide*, speech in *La Porte étroite*); a value that is modalizable in terms of the will, the obligation, the knowledge, the power from which they spring or which they imply; a value that is positive or negative with regard to the circumstances in which they appear and to the participants that they involve (in *A Thousand and One Nights*, narrative saves the narrator; in *L'Immoraliste*, it makes the narratees accomplices in a crime). Of course, these categories may be further specified and refined, but it seems to me that any theming in terms of narrative must or can use a certain number of them. Because their study has been neglected in spite of the popularity of narrative theming, in what follows I focus primarily (though by no means exclusively) on the depiction and evaluation of narrative as an object and, more specifically, on the relevant texts' views of that object's relationship to truth—but not before devoting a few pages to one element in narrative which is crucial for thematic relief in general and, in particular, for the articulation of a narrative text's attitude toward narrative.

3... The Disnarrated

We know that in certain genres and in certain periods, the representation of certain experiences, the recounting of certain actions (pertaining to, say, money, eating, excretion, sexuality) is simply taboo; and we are often aware of the unspoken agenda by which the tellability of a series of events, the narrativity of this or that mode or representation, is assessed in certain contexts. If I told a friend what I did yesterday, I would most probably not mention that I tied my shoelaces, and though I might mention that I walked for some time in the middle of the afternoon, I do not think that I would say (borrowing from Jonathan Culler): "Then, at around three o'clock, I raised my left foot two inches off the ground while swinging it forward and, displacing my center of gravity so that the foot hit the ground, heel first, strode off on the ball of my right foot, etc."[1]

More specifically, we are all familiar with the category of the unnarratable or nonnarratable, which evokes the topos of the inexpressible without being limited to it and which comprises everything that *according to a given narrative* cannot be narrated or is not worth narrating—either because it transgresses a law (social, authorial, generic, formal), or because it defies the powers of a particular narrator (or of any narrator), or because it falls below the so-called threshold of narratability (it is not sufficiently unusual or problematic: that is, interesting). I read in Chaucer's *Troilus and Criseyde*, for instance:

> But how this town com to destruction
> Ne falleth naught to purpos me to telle;
> For it were here a long digression
> Fro my matere, and yow to long to dwelle.
> But the Troian gestes, as they felle,
> In Omer, or in Dares, or in Dite,
> Whose that kan may rede hem as they write.

In Madame de La Fayette's *La Princesse de Clèves*: "One cannot express what M. de Nemours felt at that moment. To see, in the middle of the night, in the most beautiful spot in the world, a person he adored, to see her without her knowing that he saw her, and to see her thoroughly preoccupied with things related to him and to the passion she concealed from him, this has never been experienced or imagined by any other lover." And in Théophile Gautier's *Mademoiselle de Maupin*: "For a while, the conversation went from subject to subject, very witty, very cheerful, and very lively, and that is why we will not give an account of it; we fear that it would lose too much in the transcription. The looks, the tone, the fire in the language and gestures, the thousand ways of pronouncing one word, all that wit similar to the froth of Champagne wine that bubbles and evaporates at once, are things that are impossible to fix and reproduce."

Of course, as my first example should suggest, one narrative's unnarratable can very well be another's narratable, just as what is inappropriate in one context may be *de rigueur* in another. Much fiction derives some of its force from representing what is widely considered unrepresentable and from making narratively interesting what is commonly viewed as entirely lacking in interest (Samuel Beckett comes to mind as exemplary); in certain contexts, tying one's shoelaces may be strange, uncommon, dangerous, or amusing and therefore worth reporting; and, as the Russian Formalists showed, defamiliarization—making strange and thus artistically potent—often depends on detailing what is taken for granted, focusing on the specifics of our ordinary engagement in the world, and going below the accepted minimum level of functional relevance.

We are also familiar with another, closely related category that may be called the unnarrated, or nonnarrated. I am not thinking of what is left unsaid by a narrative because of ignorance, stupidity, repression, or choice. Rather, I am thinking of all the frontal and lateral ellipses found in narrative and either explicitly underlined by the narrator ("I will not recount what happened during that fateful week") or inferrable from a significant lacuna in the chronology or through a retrospective filling-in: given a series of events $e_1, e_2, e_3 \ldots e_n$ occurring at time t or at times $t_1, t_2, t_3 \ldots t_n$ respectively, one of the events goes unmentioned. In *this* case, something is not told (at least for a while) not so much because of a narratorial incapacity, a tellability imperative, a "legal" imposition, but because of some narrative call for rhythm, characterization, suspense, surprise, and so on.

Finally, we are all familiar with a third category which, although linked to the unnarratable and the unnarrated, can be taken to constitute something like their opposite. Whereas the first two categories cover all the events that happen in the world represented but are, for any number of reasons, unmentionable or unmentioned, the category that most concerns me here and that I will call *disnarrated* covers all the events that *do not* happen though they could have and are nonetheless referred to (in a negative or hypothetical mode) by the narrative text.[2]

Manifestations of the disnarrated have been noted and sometimes discussed at length in narratological literature. In "Art and Technique," for example, Victor Shklovsky speaks of such devices as negative parallelism and negative (or hypothetical) comparison: "Marie proved to be more interesting than Catherine expected." Claude Bremond, criticizing the teleological orientation of the Proppian model of narrative, writes: "Let us suppose that it is no longer a matter of simply telling a story but of telling someone's story. It is impossible to elude the opposition between what happens and what could have happened. It is impossible to tell the story of Hercules at the crossroad without letting him explore, in his imagination, one road and the other." In his work on oral narrative of personal experience, William Labov underlines the importance of what he calls *comparators*, constructions referring to "unrealized" events and comparing them to "realized" ones (negatives, modals, futures, commands, and so forth): "So I says to myself, 'There's gonna be times my mother won't give me money, because we're a poor family and I can't take this every time she don't give me money.' So I say, 'Well, I just gotta fight this girl. She gonna hafta whup me. I hope she don't whup me.'" Mary Louise Pratt does the same in her study of fictional discourse. More recently, in developing an Artificial Intelligence-inspired model of narrative that gives its due to the moments of suspense and surprise, advance and delay, trickery and illumination—to the samba-like movement emblematic of plot—Marie-Laure Ryan has focused on what she calls *virtual embedded narratives*, by which she means any story-like representation produced in the mind of a character (and sometimes, but not always, having an equivalent in the narrated world external to that mind): these mental constructs include such private domains as wishes, intents, and obligations; they do not merely reflect actual events but also delineate virtual ones.[3]

For me, and to put it again most generally, terms, phrases, and passages that consider what did not or does not take place ("this could've happened but didn't"; "this didn't happen but could've") constitute the disnarrated, whether they pertain to the narrator's vision ("You will suppose that it was the people from the inn, their servants, and the brigands of whom we spoke. . . . You will suppose that this little army will set upon Jacques and his master, that there will be a bloody skirmish, cudgel blows exchanged, pistol shots fired; and it lies entirely within my power to make all of that happen; but farewell the truth of the story") or whether they relate to the vision of a character ("I could easily have been introduced to the secret of even greater interior beauties; but I did not ask to see whether the splendors of the shirt corresponded to those of the skirt"). I am thus referring to alethic expressions of presumed impossibility or unrealized possibility ("Joan thinks that x is possible but x does not take place"), deontic expressions of (observed) prohibition, epistemic expressions of ignorance, ontologic expressions of nonexistence, purely imagined worlds, desired worlds, or intended worlds, unfulfilled expectations, unwarranted beliefs, failed attempts, crushed hopes, erroneous suppositions and false calculations, and so forth. Eleanor could have married Mr. Slope or Bertie Stanhope, but it was not destined to be. Sarrasine, going to his first rendezvous with Zambinella, hopes for "a dimly-lit room, his mistress crouching by the fire, a jealous rival near at hand, death and love, secrets exchanged in heart-to-heart whispers, perilous kisses"; but his expectations turn out to be foolish. Eveline decides to elope but, at the last moment, changes her mind. Bel-Ami muses every night: "He imagined a magnificent adventure of love which brought him, all at once, to the fulfillment of his hopes. He married the daughter of a banker or a great lord, met in the street and conquered at first sight"; this is not quite what happens to him. He has just seduced Clotilde: "How easy and unexpected it had been! Until then, he had imagined that, to approach and conquer one of these creatures he so much desired, infinite attentions were necessary, interminable waits, a skillful siege made up of gallantries, words of love, sighs, and presents. And suddenly, at the slightest of attacks, the first one he met gave way to him, so quickly that it left him dumbfounded." He promises himself to reimburse his mistress but does not do it; he wrongly imagines that Langremont is an excellent marksman; he thinks that M. de Marelle will treat him poorly, but the opposite takes place.

If the disnarrated pertains to narration, it has equivalents in the domains of description ("This bed could have been covered with roses but it was not")[4] and argumentation ("I could invoke Susan's behavior but I will invoke her work"). Similarly, if the disnarrated pertains to what could have happened or what could happen, if it relates to what is told, it finds a homolog at the level of telling: everything which, in a narrative, designates the narrating modes that could have been or could be adopted to depict what takes place ("I prefer to use direct instead of indirect discourse"). Furthermore, the mere negative depiction of a situation or event ("Warren did not close the door" rather than "Warren left the door open"; "Elizabeth did not answer" rather than "Elizabeth remained silent") does not constitute an instance of the disnarrated. Neither does a phrase like "Joshua closed the window": though it means "Joshua did not leave the window open," it in no way indicates that the character could have left the window alone. More generally, and for similar reasons, the contraries, contradictories, and "complementaries" of a given action are not necessarily disnarrated: there is nothing in "Paul wrote quickly" that implies a possibility such as "Paul did not write quickly," "Paul wrote at a moderate speed," or "Paul did not write at all." The disnarrated, which can pertain to the future, the present, or the past, which can reveal itself as such after a few lines or four hundred pages, and which can be explicit ("Like everyone else, I believed that Victor could have won but he lost") or implicit ("Isabelle got up laboriously to explain her reservations but this effort killed her"), is disnarrated only relative to a given diegesis, and only if it designates in that diegesis a possibility that remains unrealized. In other words, the contents of a dream, the components of a hallucination or delirium, can be disnarrated only if they are given as real possibilities in the relevant diegesis.

Like the unnarratable and the unnarrated, the disnarrated is clearly not essential to narrative. It need not figure in capsule reports of baseball games, for instance: *"Dodgers 6, Pirates 3. Rick Honeycutt struck out 20 batters in $8\frac{1}{3}$ innings and Mickey Hatcher drove in two runs with a homer and two other hits to lead host Los Angeles over Pittsburgh. Honeycutt (1–1) also drove in a run with a squeeze bunt in a three-run fourth inning."* It plays no role in many a news story: "Both houses of the Louisiana Legislature have passed legislation requiring that warnings of explicit lyrics be placed on record album covers and forbidding the sale of such records to minors." And it is absent from the famous and exemplary "I came, I saw, I conquered." Perhaps this is so because narrative is primarily concerned with what happened rather than what might have happened. Nevertheless, the insistence with which the disnarrated appears in countless "natural" narratives (narratives occurring more or less spontaneously in everyday conversation) as well as in fictional and historical discourse points to its narrative pertinence and significance.

Indeed, the disnarrated can fulfill numerous and varied functions which are not unique to it. For example, like metalinguistic statements, direct addresses to the reader, or passages devoted to pure description, it can become a rhythmic instrument by regularly slowing down narrative speed, the presentation of what takes place. Since it frequently consists of hopes, desires, imaginings and ponderings, unreasonable expectations, and incorrect beliefs; since it depicts what is not but might be and is often linked to carelessness, ignorance, or limitations resulting from some psychological trauma or obsession, it can function as a characterization device ("A less truthful man might have been tempted into the subsequent creation of a vision in the form of resurgent memory; a less sane man might have believed in such a creation; but Silas was both sane and honest"; "Wash had never tried to enter the big house, even though he believed that if he had, Sutpen would have received him, permitted him. 'But I ain't going to give no black nigger the chance to tell me I can't go nowhere,' he said to himself"). It can also help to define a narrator, his or her narratee, and their relationship. Thus, the narrator may emphasize his or her power by multiplying and underscoring the lines of development that could have been adopted: "It depends only on me to make you wait a year, two years, three years, for the story of Jacques's loves, by separating him from his master and making each meet with whatever accidents take my fancy. What prevents me from having the master marry and be a cuckold? from sending Jacques off to the colonies? from leading his master there? from bringing both of them back to France on the same ship? How easy it is to make up tales!" Similarly, the narratee may be shown imagining what he or she would do if involved in the situations described. The disnarrated can, moreover, help to create suspense and to articulate the narrative in hermeneutic terms (in detective novels, for instance, the possible solutions and false solutions it introduces are contrasted with the real ones); more generally, it makes explicit the logic at work in narrative whereby, as Claude Bremond emphasized,[5] every narrative function opens an alternative, a set of possible directions, and every narrative progresses by following certain directions as opposed to others: the disnarrated or choices not made, roads not taken, possibilities not actualized, goals not reached.

But as these comments should suggest, the most important function of the disnarrated is probably a rhetorical and interpretive one (the model of plot recently proposed by Marie-Laure Ryan and the remarks of William Labov on comparators underline, in fact, the link between narrativity and unrealized sequences).[6] When the disnarrated relates to a narrator's vision, it foregrounds ways of creating a world, of conceiving a situation, of exploiting this norm or rejecting that convention, and it carries some such message as "This narrative is valuable because it develops in a different and more interesting manner." When it relates to a character's vision, it underlines the quality of the narrated itself rather than the value of its construction: "This narrative is worth narrating because *it* could have been otherwise, because *it* usually is otherwise, because *it* was *not* otherwise." Indeed, the vision to which the disnarrated refers as well as its content (material or spiritual, alethic or epistemic), the relative frequency with which it appears, and the relative amount of space it occupies characterize in part certain narrative options. Thus, the realist text and, more generally, mimetic fiction resort to the disnarrated mainly through a character in order to contrast the true with the lifelike and to show themselves steeped in reality rather than fantasy. The overtly metafictional narrative, on the contrary, resorts to it mainly through a narrator in order to multiply signs of arbitrariness and contingency and in order to insist on the text's own artificiality.

If it underlines the nature of a narrative (or, at least, the nature that a narrative claims to have or shows an inclination for), the disnarrated also underlines its meaning or, at least, some of its themes. Like any other textual component, it can illustrate one or several of these themes. Given the variety of contents that it can designate, given too the impossibility of specifying the intension or extension of a theme, and given the great suppleness of those textual factors and operations that foster the relating of a theme and a text, it is, of course, impossible to characterize the infinitely large set of themes that the disnarrated can express. Still, there are indubitable links between the disnarrated and topoi, whether the former serves to reject an artifice that conceals itself for the benefit of a self-declared one (this is what happens in the metafictional text) or whether it serves to refuse this convention or that commonplace or else to designate a situation, a series of events, as banal and—so to speak—as already topical (this is what happens in the realist text).[7] There are also thematic fields for which the disnarrated has many affinities. I am thinking, for example, of the class of themes that somehow imply the notion "unrealized" (the theme of missed occasions, lost illusions, unjustified ambitions) and, more generally, of the class of themes governed by contrasts and contraries (lifelikeness and reality, appearance and being, determinism and freedom, imagination and perception, and so on). Finally, and most relevantly, there is the theme of narrative itself and, in particular, the opposition between good and bad narratives or, rather, between narratives that are adequate to the truth and narratives that are not.

It is perhaps primarily through its role in the constitution of thematic relief that the disnarrated contributes to the meaning of narratives and to its communication. In the first place, as a unit of commentary it plays a part in thematic focalization, in the accentuation of certain themes (we know that, all other things being equal, narrative elements that are commented on—and, therefore, the themes they represent—are in the foreground, relative to those elements unaccompanied by commentary); it does so, moreover, in a particularly clear way since it always figures the virtual as opposed to the actual, what is abandoned instead of adopted. Furthermore, it plays a part in thematic designation, in the individualization of themes, since it signals that certain of their manifestations are abandoned for the sake of certain others, that certain possible articulations are not selected, that certain characteristics are too hackneyed to be taken seriously. In *Madame Bovary* (which I pick for its exemplariness, though I could have picked *La Princesse de Clèves, Candide, La Peste*, or *A la recherche du temps perdu*), it is in great part thanks to the disnarrated (thanks to all the romantic and sentimental stories imagined by the protagonist) that the theme of good narrative—disinterested, disciplined, courageous, exact—is underscored.

The disnarrated guides reading by constituting a model that allows texts better to define themselves, to specify and emphasize the meanings they wish to communicate, and to designate the values they develop and aspire to.

4... Singular Narrative

La Princesse de Clèves opens by asserting the tellability, the exceptional nature of the situations and events it depicts: "Magnificence and gallantry never appeared in France with such brilliance as in the last years of the reign of Henry II."[1] The king's court is a privileged locus of worldliness in which pretense rules ("what seems the case is almost never true," 51) and political or amorous intrigues multiply: "Ambition and gallantry were the soul of that court and kept men and women equally busy. There were so many interests and so many different cabals, and the ladies had such a part in them, that love was always mixed with politics and politics with love. No one was tranquil, or indifferent. People thought of improving their position, of pleasing, of serving or harming; they felt neither boredom nor idleness; and they were always busy with pleasures or with plots" (33). Constituted in the main by such plots, Henry's court generates abundant narrative material. Indeed, at least one characterization of that court by the narrator would apply just as well to narrative and its regulated excitement: "a kind of agitation without disorder" (34).

Madame de La Fayette's text itself is a patchwork of narratives. I do not simply mean that, like indefinitely many novels or tales, *La Princesse de Clèves* can be said to result from the linkage of (simple) stories through such operations as conjoining, embedding, and alternation.² Nor am I merely pointing to the fact that—again like indefinitely many novels or tales—*La Princesse de Clèves* includes many disnarrated stretches, story-like representations of what could have happened but did not, of what might have been but was not: M. de Nemours could have gone to England and might have married Queen Elizabeth but he decided not to (26); the heroine wanted to tell her mother how she felt toward M. de Nemours but Mme de Chartres was ill (66); M. de Clèves never recounted his wife's confession to him though he could have (173).³ Rather, I am referring specifically to one compositional aspect of the text that has become a *locus classicus* of criticism: the insertion of four largely autonomous narratives into the main narrative. And, more generally, I am thinking of the fact that in the world of the novel most of the action consists of language acts, and many of these are narrative acts.⁴

The four interpolated narratives exhibit important differences as well as meaningful similarities. On the one hand, two of them—the first and the third—focus on events from a relatively distant past (the beginning of Henry's passion for Diane de Poitiers; the story of Anne Boleyn), whereas the other two relate contemporary situations (the deceptiveness of Mme de Tournon; the multiple and dangerous liaisons of the Vidame de Chartres)—or, to put it in a way that relies on extratextual data, the first and third narratives have a "historical" subject, while the second and fourth have a "fictional" one. The former, which are told by women (Mme de Chartres and Mary Stuart), are significantly shorter than the latter, which are recounted by men (M. de Clèves and the Vidame); and their concision, like their penchant for history, may well have something to do with the sex of their narrator: after all, La Fayette adopts a historical frame for her short novel, and the only actual writer she mentions by name is a woman, Marguerite de Navarre (102–3). Furthermore, the first three narratives—heterodiegetic ones—have a female protagonist and are addressed to the novel's heroine by a narrator who is superior to her in status and who functions as her protector (her mother, a queen, and her husband). The fourth—homodiegetic—narrative has a male protagonist and is addressed to a male narratee (M. de Nemours) by a narrator who is his peer. Finally, if the first three narratives are told primarily in response to the heroine's desire to know, the last one springs from the narrator's wish to have his narratee perform a task for him.

On the other hand, all four narratives, in spite of their autonomy, are thematically linked to the main narrative: they all illustrate the fickleness of lovers and their duplicity, the precariousness of love, the ravages that passion produces and the pains that it inflicts. Moreover, they all insist on the discrepancies between appearance and being, official story and inside story, an insistence that their very textual situation (they are intercalated, inside stories themselves) can only reinforce. All four also contribute to the possible motivations of Mme de Clèves as well as to the forward movement of the novel's plot, and all four exemplify various aspects of narrative as product or process and help to emphasize its powerful effects.

The first interpolated narrative is introduced soon after Mme de Clèves tells her mother of her admiration for M. de Nemours, without realizing what Mme de Chartres quickly surmises: the heroine is already falling in love with the prince. Mme de Clèves knows little about love. In particular, she cannot understand the attachment of the king to Diane de Poitiers, duchess of Valentinois, who is much older than he is, was his father's mistress, and often proves unfaithful. The text stages elaborately the contract between narrator and narratee underlying the very existence of narrative and stressing its transactional nature: Mme de Clèves wants to learn and asks for a story; Mme de Chartres does not want to recount old tales, as so many older women do, but hopes to enlighten, guide, and warn her daughter. She finally accedes to the wishes of the heroine (who, at the end of the narrative, expresses gratitude) and tells her Diane's real story while showing how the past illuminates the present. Mme de Chartres's narrative touches upon many topics: the mutability of passion, for instance (52, 57), the unworthiness of Henry's love (though it has lasted for over twenty years, the costs in compromise and suffering have been great), the effect that physical separation can have on lovers' feelings (out of sight, out of mind!), the cabals of court life, the unreliability of appearances. It also exploits an important theme in the novel: that of telling and not telling, of speaking, not speaking, and being "spoken" (*être parlé*) or spoken about. In particular, it cautions against revealing one's amorous adventures: M. de Taix was disgraced because he was indiscreet; later, the Vidame de Chartres, who proves overly talkative on at least three occasions (36, 120-21, 167), meets a similar fate. In contrast, it praises those who manage to keep their feelings private and to escape (onomastically) the narratives of others: "The duke of Orleans ... loved one of the most beautiful women in the court and he was loved by her. I will not tell you her name because, since that time, she has behaved so discreetly and has even hidden so carefully the passion that she had for this prince that she deserves to keep her reputation" (55). Of course, Mme de Clèves will successfully avoid becoming an object of gossip, and her character will remain unsullied.

The second and longest narrative is told by M. de Clèves to his wife. Her mother has recently died after warning her against *galanterie*, and the heroine, who has lost her main protectress, is now aware of her feelings for M. de Nemours and desperately trying to retain her virtue. When she learns of the sudden death of Mme de Tournon, a beautiful young widow known for an extraordinary determination never to remarry, the news increases her distress. But M. de Clèves, who greatly admired the widow himself, says that she does not deserve any pity: "Women are incomprehensible" (73); Mme de Tournon was a hypocrite; she had a liaison both with his good friend Sancerre and with Estouteville and had promised each to marry him. Apart from foreshadowing the heroine's own decision never to remarry and insisting on the illusive nature of appearances and the scandalous consequences of passion, M. de Clèves's narrative is notable in at least two respects. First, the narrator tells his wife what he told Sancerre when the latter felt that Mme de Tournon's affection for him seemed to wane: "I said to him . . . that if she did not have the strength to marry him or if she confessed that she loved someone else, he should neither get angry nor complain but keep his regard for her and his gratitude. 'I am giving advice,' I said to him, 'that I would follow myself; for sincerity affects me so that I believe that if my mistress, and even my wife, confessed to me that she was attracted to someone, I would feel sad without being bitter. I would drop the role of lover or husband to adore and pity her'" (80). Mme de Clèves's famous confession is not far off. Second, the contagious potential of narrative is foregrounded. Thus, M. de Clèves recounts how M. d'Anville told him a story that he in turn told Sancerre, who recounted it to Mme de Tournon, who related it to the narrator's sister-in-law, who repeated it to him word for word (76–77). Moreover, M. de Clèves, who heard Sancerre's tale of unhappy and jealous love, soon functions as its narrator and later will become the protagonist of a similarly poignant tale. Narrative leads to narrative, and one narrative role leads to another.

In the third and shortest narrative, Mary Stuart recounts the life of Anne Boleyn to a group of ladies that includes Mme de Clèves. The latter has learned that M. de Nemours may marry Elizabeth of England, but she feels obliged not to show any interest in the subject. Instead, she often asks about her rival's attributes. When she sees a particularly beautiful portrait of her, she cannot help saying that it must be flattering. Mary Stuart disagrees, pointing out that the queen's mother, Anne Boleyn, was an extremely handsome woman and proceeding to tell her sad story. The narrative not only evokes its narrator's own fate, links individual intrigues with historical change—the Church of England stems from Henry's anger at the pope (104)—and, once again, underscores the perils of illicit love and the way male passion dies when satisfied; it also rectifies certain mistakes—Anne Boleyn was born in England, not in France (102)—and proves most instructive (105). Just as important, perhaps, it immediately precedes the scene in which M. de Nemours purloins a small portrait of the heroine, who witnesses the action and yet keeps silent.

The final narrative may be the richest in consequences. Told by the Vidame in order to convince M. de Nemours to help him recover a compromising letter, it brings to light his fickleness, deceptiveness, and lack of discretion. Like the first narrative, it is framed by a detailed contract scene: M. de Nemours agrees to help when he realizes that the heroine may think the letter is his. Like the second, it starts a chain of narrative contagions: M. de Nemours will tell Mme de Clèves the Vidame's story, and later (by mentioning her confession), he will be guilty of indiscretion himself. Like the third, it is tied to the heroine's feelings of love and jealousy (she did believe that the compromising letter was Nemours's). In fact, it leads to the first tête-à-tête between the novel's two protagonists, to an intimate nocturnal scene in which they reconstruct and rewrite the misplaced letter, to the heroine's confession (in an effort to protect herself against her feelings), and perhaps to her final decision not to yield to her passion (147–48).

In a similar way, the many other narrative acts that make up the novel's action—from Mme de Chartres's didactic sessions with her daughter through Mary Stuart's reports on M. de Nemours's English prospects to the Vidame's retelling of the heroine's confession (27, 88–90, 167)—motivate the characters, move the plot forward, and shed light on the possible functions of narration: narrative can inform, guide, mislead, provide relief, or kill (cf. esp. 27, 67, 158–59, 176, 210). These acts also underline narrative's remarkable capacity to spread: for example, M. de Nemours overhears Mme de Clèves's confession and cannot help reporting it to the Vidame, who recounts it to Mme de Martigues, who tells it to Mary Stuart, who relates it to the heroine. Most of all, they foreground the opposition between being and appearance by emphasizing the dissimilarity between the *vrai* and the *vraisemblable*, what is true (however unlikely it may be) and what is plausible (but not necessarily the case).

Two sequences of events in particular are noteworthy. In the first the king, who is discussing horoscopes with members of his court, states that he has not given any credit to prognostications since a famous astrologer told him a very unlikely story about his future, predicting that he would be killed in a duel (98). But Henry has just made peace with the king of Spain, and even if he had not, he doubts that they would meet in single combat (99). Besides, he is widely acknowledged to be the best jouster in France (17, 184). Everyone around him agrees that the prediction was foolish (99). Now, to celebrate his daughter's wedding and his sister's, the king decides to organize a jousting tournament. It is a magnificent spectacle, and as it is coming to an end, Henry insists on one final contest with the count of Montgomery—against the queen's wishes and the count's. He is accidentally killed, and the High Constable, remembering the prediction, understands that it has been fulfilled (185–86). However unlikely a story may seem, it can be true. To behave according to plausible schemata exclusively can lead to death.

In the second, M. de Clèves—who thinks that Nemours is going to Coulommiers to see the heroine in his absence—asks one of his men to watch his rival and to report on his activities. The man tells Clèves that Nemours was in the Coulommiers garden two nights in a row, once for the entire night. Two stories are possible. The unlikely one—which we know to be true and which the Princess tells her husband (200–207)—is that Nemours went to Coulommiers, surreptitiously entered the garden twice, and spent a whole night there but never managed even to speak with the heroine. The likely one—which M. de Clèves believes too quickly and which kills him (210–11, 212, 216)—is that the Princess was unfaithful. The lesson is clear. Implausible sequences of events can happen. To reject their possibility and to be guided by convention can prove fatal.

As is well known, La Fayette's novel was criticized for its implausibility when it first appeared.[5] Specifically, its most famous scene—that of the heroine's confession to her husband—was thought to be thoroughly lacking in verisimilitude (and thoroughly out of place in a work of fiction). The criticism may have been well founded in its seventeenth-century context, but the fact remains that the confession does not necessarily spring from an uncontrolled melodramatic imagination; nor does it represent a failure of psychological insight; nor is it an ad hoc device to move the plot forward. On the contrary, it is prepared for and motivated by much that precedes it (I have already noted, for example, how both the second interpolated narrative and the fourth announce it). Yet rather than drawing attention to its plausibility, the text repeatedly emphasizes its unlikeliness, its strangeness, its singularity. Before acknowledging to M. de Clèves that someone else is in love with her and that she is afraid of her own feelings, the Princess tells him: "I am going to make a confession that no one ever made to her husband" (152); M. de Clèves thinks that, by confessing, she gave him "the greatest proof of loyalty" a woman ever gave her spouse (154); and M. de Nemours, who is secretly following their conversation, believes the *aveu* to be an "extraordinary remedy" (155). After her husband leaves, the heroine reflects upon "the singularity of a confession" for which she finds no precedent (157). As for Nemours, he thinks that what he has heard is so exceptional that he cannot help reporting it to the Vidame (though without mentioning Mme de Clèves's name), and he is not sure whether it was not a dream (158–59, 162). Still later, when the story of the confession becomes the talk of Henry's court, the Princess instantly knows the identity of its unnamed protagonist, and she accuses M. de Clèves of having betrayed her trust: "There is not in the world another adventure similar to mine; there is not another woman capable of the same thing.

Chance cannot have led anyone to invent it; it was never contrived; and this idea could never occur to anyone else but me" (175).

From beginning to end, the heroine is placed under the sign of the incomparable (26–28) and the implausible. After M. de Clèves sees her for the first time, he is unable to speak of anything else, and the king's sister finds what he says unbelievable: "Madame told him that there was no person like the one he depicted and that, if there was, she would be known to everyone" (29–30). As the text underscores, the confession of the Princess is unique. Though like other women she comes to know the force of passion, she is "very far from resembling them" (179). Her avowal to Nemours of her love for him manifests "a sincerity that is seldom found among persons of [her] sex" (226). Finally, as the last sentence of the novel puts it, "her life, which was rather short, left inimitable examples of virtue" (243).

It would be wrong, however, to think that this incomparable being has no belief in (the powers of) the plausible. Its value is frequently undeniable, and like several other characters—M. de Clèves or the king but also Mary Stuart, who agrees that the story of the confession is *invraisemblable* (172); and M. de Nemours, who tells his sister a "likely story" to explain his presence at Coulommiers (207)—the Princess uses it to interpret her situation and regulate her behavior. For example, she finds it unlikely "that a man like Nemours . . . would be capable of a sincere and lasting attachment" (148), and she sees that she would probably be unable to resist him while remaining at the court (239). In fact, her opinion of the plausible, her fear of the plots it represents and governs (women fall prey to passion; love is not eternal; it leads to jealousy and bitterness; it brings about countless sufferings and scandals), her dislike for the roles it offers (unfaithful spouse, suspicious lover, wretched woman) combine with a strong awareness of her own singularity (a loyalty to self: she is not like others and cannot accept the parts they play) as well as with feelings of guilt (she was one of the causes of her husband's death), regard for duty (she must remain faithful to his memory and to the memory of her mother), and respect for virtue to determine her actions and shape her destiny.

Not for Mme de Clèves the all too common adulterous episode, nor, of course, the conventional tale and its "they lived happily ever after" ending. She will not be contaminated by familiar plots. She will not be expressed by them. She will not inhabit their space. Faced with plausible but ordinary stories and a unique but possible one, she opts for the latter. If she must be subject to narrative, the subject of a narrative, it will be one adequate to and worthy of her singularity, one she fashions for herself and in which she can be what she appears to be: exemplarily and inimitably virtuous.[6]

Like its protagonist, Madame de La Fayette's work knows the power of plausibility, but it self-consciously favors implausibility—not the extravagant and paradoxically conventional kind found in sentimental narratives or romances, but the kind proceeding from and productive of singular truth. The governing (esthetic) principle is, in fact, stated explicitly: "Truth is persuasive . . . even when it is not plausible" (216).[7] Though *La Princesse de Clèves* exploits commonplace forms and well-established strategies, it fashions itself as other.[8] It is neither a wonderful (fairy) tale—in spite of the important "once upon a time there was a beautiful princess" motif—nor a *précieux* romance: though it resorts to the complicated machinery of stolen portraits and misplaced letters and though it exhibits a strong inclination for linguistic superlatives, it rejects spatio-temporal exoticism and implausibilities bordering on the nonmimetic. Nor is it a *nouvelle historique* (it refuses the *vraisemblable* at crucial junctures), a tragic story (even if it exhibits many an affinity for Corneille and Racine), or a didactic account (the text denounces the follies of passion and praises reason, virtue, and self-control, but it narrates an inimitable destiny). Rather, *La Princesse de Clèves* constitutes a space for the exploration of what is or what can possibly be, however unlikely. It affirms the essential kinship between an exceptional truth and a narrative that dares to be exceptional. It aspires to function, above all, as a veraciously unique (re)presentation of an incomparable singularity. It is novel and widely regarded as the first (modern) French novel.

5... Candid Explanations

In many narratives, certain passages explain, motivate, or justify at least some of the events and situations represented and the mode of their representation. In "Jane ate because she was hungry," for instance, Jane's hunger is explicitly identified as the cause of her eating; and in "John was deliriously happy; I say 'deliriously' because he hallucinated," the choice of adverb is expressly justified. The study of explanations in a particular narrative, of their content, origin, destination, distribution, object, and form (what is explained? by whom? for whom? at what point? for what reasons? in what terms?), can obviously lead to more comprehensive descriptions of various characters (one who often explains differs from one who seldom does; one who always requires explanations differs from one who never needs them), just as it can lead to more precise distinctions among the situations and events reported (a state of affairs deemed worthy of explanation is no doubt different from one going unexplained). More interesting and crucial, such a study can help to determine the position of the narrative toward the possibility of knowledge (if I explain something, it is, presumably, because I think I know its nature), toward its own communicability (I explain something, say, because I want to be understood and I think I can be; I do not explain something because I feel there is no need for it or because it is impossible), and toward the value of different kinds of explanation, including the narrative kind.

Candide, ou l'Optimisme is a case in point.[1] Beginning with the title—which can, after all, be read as "Candide or, in other words, Optimism"—Voltaire's most famous work develops in part around the problem of meaning and interpretation and, more specifically, around attempts to answer the following two questions: what should one make of all the evil one encounters? what meaning should one ascribe to the universe? Moreover, it does not shy away from explanation: we learn why the hero is named "Candide" (137), why he goes on a walk one beautiful spring day (140), how it is that Pangloss finds some vinegar in a stable (144), and even what "the honors of sepulture" really means (192). Indeed, Jean Sareil barely exaggerates when he writes that in *Candide*, "every action will be . . . explained, either by the characters, who always seem eager to analyze their reactions, or by a general kind of commentary."[2]

I have counted 132 constructions that *explicitly* elucidate some feature of the world represented or its representation,[3] and they are quite varied in form: metalinguistic statements ("the Oreillons, inhabitants of the country," 172), prepositional phrases ("The Jew, in order to tame me, brought me to this house," 152), participial, conjunctive, or subordinate clauses ("pigs being made to be eaten, we eat pork all year," 138; "they entered a quite simple house, for the door was nothing but silver," 177; "the preachers of Surinam persecuted him because they took him for a Socinian," 186), and so on. More significantly, fifty-seven of these explanatory constructions are introduced by *car* (thirty-six), *parce que* (ten), *comme* (seven), and *puisque* (four): that is, almost half the 118 found by Pierre Haffter in all of Voltaire's tales.[4] Nor is explaining the exclusive province of one voice: Pangloss, who appears in only nine of the thirty chapters in the tale, supplies twenty-six of the 132 examples, but Candide contributes ten, Cunégonde six, Martin five, a dozen other characters one or more, and the narrator no less than seventy. Excluding the narratee (to whom seventy are addressed), the candid protagonist is, of course, the main receiver of explanatory statements: he functions as addressee for at least forty explanations (half of which come from Pangloss!), whereas Cacambo performs the role seven times, Cunégonde three, and Pangloss, Martin, and the Old Woman only twice each.

The explanations provided by Pangloss—the only character who explains something in both the first chapter and the last—are consistently ridiculous: they are tautological, incoherent, unconvincing, or flatly contradicted by events. Should Pangloss decide to establish why there is a volcano in Lisbon, he simply asserts that it could not be anywhere else (148); should he want to prove that syphilis is indispensable, he argues that without it we would not have chocolate (145); should he wish to explain why we have eyeglasses, he reasons that noses were made to wear them (138); and should he demonstrate that everything is for the best, a murderous tempest occurs (146). The other characters usually do not even bother to question and refute Pangloss's explanations. If they do ("While Candide, the baron, Pangloss, Martin, and Cacambo were relating their adventures, reasoning on the contingent and noncontingent events in this universe, disputing on the effects and the causes, on moral evil and physical evil, on freedom and necessity . . . they landed on the shore of Propontis," 217; "Candide, Martin, and Pangloss disputed sometimes about metaphysics and morality," 218), their counterarguments are not reported by the narrator: the inadequacy of Pangloss's pronouncements is obvious enough without them.[5] The dervish behaves more bluntly: he tells Pangloss to shut up and refuses to argue with him (220). Even Candide, who is full of admiration for "the greatest philosopher in Germany" and more than willing to be convinced, frequently cannot believe that Pangloss is right. His experiences point to a different conclusion (e.g., 149, 164, 179, 183), and on several occasions his common sense makes him put an end to his teacher's logorrhea ("That is admirable, said Candide, but we must get you cured," 145; "Nothing is more probable, said Candide; but, for God's sake, [get me] a little oil and wine," 148; "That is well said, answered Candide, but we must cultivate our garden," 221).

The inanity of Pangloss's explanations is a function of their nature and object. Pangloss never considers the immediate causes or effects of a particular event, though he is always eager to provide its original cause and ultimate effect. He never wonders about the possible meaning of a specific state of affairs; rather, he tirelessly expounds the meaning of the universe. In spite of his sensuality, he is concerned not with the physical world (which the characters experience) but with a metaphysical one (which they do not). As the attributive discourse in the text emphasizes ("It is demonstrated, *he would say*," 138; "All this was indispensable, *the one-eyed doctor would reply*," 146; "*Pangloss would sometimes say to Candide*," 221), he frequently repeats himself.[6] Indeed, as he favors a priori reasons and arguments by design, he always starts from the same premises and reaches the same conclusions, regardless of circumstance. Notwithstanding the diversity of events occurring around him—anything can happen in *Candide*, and almost everything does—he never modifies his line; and his explanations, even if well formed, are condemned to uselessness, because their connection with reality must be purely coincidental. Pangloss does not explain because he knows, nor does he explain in order to be helpful. He explains, paradoxically, because he does not (care to) know and whether or not an explanation is called for. He explains, without really explaining, because he is a professional explainer who can no more abandon metaphysical argumentation than refrain from speaking. His name is, of course, revealing ("all tongue"), and so is the fact that he loses an eye (his vision is partial at best), that syphilis severely affects his speech apparatus ("the mouth askew, the teeth black, and speaking from the throat, tormented by a violent cough, and spitting out a tooth with every effort," 143), and that he admires Homer and an oral tradition depending on a given set of themes and formulas.[7]

The very form of the explanations contributed by Pangloss underlines their inadequacy. In the first place, his complicated and often impenetrable syntax, as well as his penchant for putting forth a tangle of reasons (on 138, he provides five in less than thirteen lines; on 148, four in just four lines), betrays the confusion of his thinking. Often, as Pierre Haffter points out, "the reasons advanced by Pangloss are shown to be absurd through the immediate addition of other causal, temporal, or hypothetical subordinate clauses. For the explanation to make sense, numerous other circumstances first have to be realized."[8] More tellingly, perhaps, Pangloss's favorite introductory term for an explanatory phrase is *car* ("for"): it appears in over half of his contributions (fifteen times). His very first explanation begins with it ("It is demonstrated, he would say, that things cannot be otherwise: for, everything being made for an end, everything is necessarily for the best end," 138), and so does his final one ("All events are linked in the best of possible worlds. For, after all, if you had not been kicked out of a beautiful castle . . . you would not be here eating preserved citrons and pistachio-nuts," 221). Now *car* does not introduce the cause of a given event so much as the reason for an assertion; it does not explain circumstances in the world so much as statements about them. Typically, Pangloss is interested in words rather than facts. His bias is emphasized by his neglect of certain other explanatory constructions: *parce que*, which—in contradistinction with *car*—presumably sets forth the effective causes of a situation, is used only once by Pangloss; participial clauses, which link causality to temporality and (immediate) circumstance, are chosen three times less frequently than *car*; and *comme*, which not only is related to *comment* — to a "how" rather than a "why" — but also makes temporal meanings converge with causal ones, is never selected by the metaphysician.

Toward the end of the tale, Pangloss himself acknowledges the vapidity of his explanations and their irrelevance to the "real world." When Candide asks him whether he thought that everything was for the best even as he was being hanged, he replies: "I still abide by my first feeling . . . for, after all, I am a philosopher: it does not become me to recant" (216). And in the final chapter, the narrator confirms that the philosopher does not believe in what he says but merely thinks that he must say it: "Pangloss confessed that he had always suffered horribly; but, having once maintained that everything went wonderfully well, he still maintained it and did not believe a word of it" (219). Like all those who abandon physics for metaphysics, forget facts and remember words, insist on speaking of order even when they see disorder, disregard the world but assign it a meaning, Pangloss is incorrigible. Yet life and Candide's garden have their effect on him. Whereas he resorts to *car* no fewer than eleven times before he is hanged, he uses it only four times in the last four chapters; and although he maintains to the very end that all events are connected in this best of possible worlds, he maintains it only *sometimes* (221).

If Pangloss is above all interested in explaining why the world in which he lives is the best possible, and if he never wastes an opportunity to do so, the other characters in *Candide*—excluding the protagonist—seldom have recourse to explicit modes of explanation: not one of them uses *car* more than once, and together they produce fewer explanatory statements (twenty-five) than Pangloss does. When they do, it is to elucidate for their interlocutors specific events or states of affairs rather than to "demonstrate" pointless propositions for no one in particular. Paquette, for example, tells Candide why she became the mistress of a doctor (201); Cunégonde explains some of her feelings (157) and some of her actions (152); Pococuranté makes clear why he sleeps with two of his servants (204); Martin himself, whose pessimism rivals Pangloss's optimism but is partly grounded in reality, explains why he took a proofreader's job (189), why Europe is teeming with paid assassins (187), and what a given expression means (192). And when the Old Woman, who has considerable experience and ultimately moves Candide's little group to action (219), ventures an explanation for the general statement she has cautiously formulated, it is through a series of questions: "This ridiculous weakness is perhaps one of our most disastrous penchants: for is there anything more idiotic than wanting continually to carry a load that one always wants to throw on the ground? to hold one's being in detestation and to cling to one's being? In a word, to caress the serpent that devours us till he has eaten up our heart?" (163). In other terms, though most characters in *Candide*, including such highly positive ones as Cacambo or the King of Eldorado, do not shun explanatory observations, their aims in using them are always limited: formal explanation need not be ridiculous; it is quite acceptable when it fulfills a practical or social function.

Of all the characters in *Candide*, the protagonist probably has the most interesting, though not the most idiosyncratic, attitude toward explanation. Like his teacher Pangloss, whom he initially parrots rather well ("There is no effect without cause, answered Candide modestly: everything is necessarily linked, and arranged for the best," 142), Candide shows a definite penchant for *car*: he uses it seven times, and it helps to introduce his first three and his last three explanatory statements (140, 143, 157, 190, 192, 196). Moreover, fully half of his explanations pertain to such general problems as the fundamental goodness of nature (174), the essential character of human beings (190), and the identity of the best possible world (143, 157, 177). Unlike Pangloss, however, and with one or possibly two exceptions (177, 190), Candide grounds his explanations in experience or common sense: he cannot say he likes the King of the Bulgarians, because he has never laid eyes on him (140); uncorrupted nature must be good, since the Oreillons were nice to him as soon as they learned that he was no Jesuit (174); everything is for the best, since he is far more touched by one man's kindness than by the harshness of other human beings (143). Furthermore, Candide explains with the hope of convincing his interlocutors: explanation, for him, has a communicative function. In this respect, his (naive) reliance on *puisque*, the only other explanatory term he uses, is revealing because *puisque* not only indicates the point of departure of a particular line of reasoning but also presupposes a desire for one's receiver's acquiescence.

If Candide initially lacks experience, he is straightforward and free from bias (in a word, candid). He stands outside convention, being after all an *enfant naturel*, an illegitimate child (137). Besides, though innocent, he shows a fine capacity for comparison and evaluation: "He had a rather sound judgment" (137). His conclusions, unlike Pangloss's, are not always already given. He is not always sure that he lives in the best of all possible worlds: "Cunégonde is dead! Ah! best of worlds, where are you?" (144); "If this is the best of possible worlds, what then are the others?" (149); "Everything is fine, granted; but I confess that it is very cruel to have lost Miss Cunégonde and to be spitted by some Oreillons" (173). And his adventures—like those of others—sometimes lead him to argue that he does not: "We are going into another universe, said Candide; surely it must be there that everything is fine. For I must confess that one could moan a little about what happens in ours both physically and morally" (157). Finally, relative to Pangloss, Candide provides few explanations (ten). At the beginning he explains very little—twice in nine chapters—because he does not know; in chapters 23 to 29 he does not explain because he cares to know (through most of the tale he asks a lot of questions); and, in the final chapter, he need not explain because he knows ("I know also, said Candide, that we must cultivate our garden," 221), and what he knows—a particular truth rather than a general one, "*our* garden" and not "*one's* garden"—is so evident that it requires no explanation. The work in the garden and its results prove to be more eloquent than any formal proof.

The basic opposition within which *Candide* develops, however, is not so much between the protagonist and his teacher—the character who learns and does not need to explain, and the character who never learns yet will always explain—but rather between Pangloss and the narrator (who, etymologically and narratively, is "the one who knows").[9] The latter does not hesitate to specify the cause or effect of some events in the world—he or she contributes more explanations (seventy) than all the characters put together—but refuses to elucidate the meaning of the world, consistently preferring a "short causality" over one presuming to establish first causes and last effects.[10] Empirical knowledge of the world—for the narrator, the only world there is—constitutes the basis for all clarifications: why does Candide feel desperately sad? because he has lost a fortune (185); why does he suddenly have many friends? because he is wearing an enormous diamond ring (190); why do people hate Don Fernando? because he is insufferable (164). The ordinariness of what the narrator chooses to explain and the modesty of the explanations underline the absurdity of those who pretend to solve nonmathematical problems "by A plus B, minus C, divided by Z" (190).

The narrator's first explanatory statement is cautious: "He had a rather sound judgment together with the most unaffected mind; it is, I believe, for this reason that he was called Candide" (137). Subsequent explanations are just as limited in scope, and their formal variety is in harmony with the variety of events and situations presented. If the protagonist depends exclusively on *car* and *puisque* and if Pangloss relies mainly on *car*, the narrator resorts to no fewer than twenty-two different explanatory formulas,[11] including *car* six times (that is, in fewer than 9 percent of the cases), *comme* as often as *car, parce que* seven times, and the participial clause—the favorite mode by far—sixteen times.

On the one hand, then, the narrator's explanatory arsenal is remarkable; she or he knows the many forms elucidation can take and in several passages even makes it clear that explanations are very easy to invent. How is it, for instance, that Cacambo speaks Peruvian? Well, everyone knows that he was born in Tucuman (176). On the other hand, the narrator prefers expressions that emphasize particular circumstances and bear on specific facts rather than general propositions.

The narrator trusts the adaptability of language to the world: one can say or write what one thinks (207), and a character's name—Candide or Pangloss but also Pococuranté, Thunder-ten-tronckh, or Cunégonde—signals comically the harmony between words and things. The narrator also has such confidence in the mere parading of facts and the power of whatever evidence it provides that he or she does not always attempt to give them a foundation or to link them in explicitly causal ways. Whereas Pangloss likes to connect propositions that have little or nothing in common through an array of (pseudo)logical operations, the narrator often dispenses with the signs of explanation and simply describes what happens: "The snow fell in great flakes. Candide, chilled to the bone, dragged himself the next day toward the next town" (139); "He wrote well and knew arithmetic perfectly. Jacques the Anabaptist made him his bookkeeper" (145); "He was almost beside himself with joy. He embraced his dear friend" (208). The narrator is not alone: most of the characters, including the protagonist, frequently rely on what is at most an implicit formulation of causality (e.g., 152, 162, 163). Facts speak for themselves. If they form a relevant chain, it will be obvious to any sensible human being; if they are meaningful, their meaning will be clear.[12] To ask whether or not everything is for the best in the best of all possible worlds is foolish because such a general question cannot be answered on the basis of our particular experience. In contrast, certain events are incontrovertible, and the mere recording of them leads to firm conclusions. There are natural disasters (in *Candide*, one tempest and two earthquakes) and diseases (syphilis, the plague) that kill some innocent people and spare some criminals; and there are many more evils created by human beings: wars and inquisitions, thievery and piracy, exploitation and slavery. Yet human beings are not doomed to be the victims of nature (Candide and his little group, like the old Turk and his family, prosper on the shores of Propontis); and though many of them are "liars, cheats, brigands, perfidious, ungrateful, weak, fickle, cowardly, envious, gluttonous, drunk, miserly, ambitious, bloodthirsty, slanderous, debauched, fanatical, hypocritical, and stupid" (189), at least some are worthy of affection. Candide is a fair master (166, 184) with a sweet temper, a sound judgment, and a pure heart (137, 164); Cacambo is a very good man (184), a fine friend (211), and a prudent and faithful servant (218); Jacques, the Anabaptist, is honest and kind (143); even Pangloss proves his loyalty to and gratitude for his pupil (244); and Brother Giroflée becomes an honorable fellow (221). Somehow, life with all its hardships must be worth living: "I have seen a prodigious number of persons who held their existence in abhorrence, but I saw only twelve who voluntarily put an end to their misery" (163). Besides, we must cultivate our garden.

To explain *why* something is what it is can be helpful, but the explanation provided, like the "something" explained, must be clear, concrete, and practical. It should not express the obvious—unless such obviousness is pointed or helps to strengthen the bonds between addresser and addressee—nor should it rest on implausible and ill-defined postulates.[13] To recount *what* occurs (not excluding the contingent or the unexplainable) and *how* it does is usually more than adequate. There are, in fact, thirteen uses of *comment* ("how") in the thirty chapter titles of *Candide*, four uses of *arriver* ("happen"), and four of *advenir* ("befall"). Furthermore, the text is from the beginning under the sign of narrative ("There was in Westphalia . . . ," 137) and consists, in large part, of narratives—by Candide, Cunégonde, the Old Woman, Cacambo, Giroflée, and even Pangloss, not to mention the six fallen kings attending the carnival in Venice and the many people who, on board ship or in Surinam (164, 185) tell their story to the protagonist. Ultimately, *Candide* contrasts two ways of addressing the human condition, two kinds of logic, two modes of discourse. There is, on the one hand, the metaphysics espoused by Pangloss (but rejected by the dervish—"the best philosopher in Turkey"; 218—who has no patience for futile arguments about the unknowable first causes and final effects of problematic states of affairs). On the other hand, there is the kind of narrative favored by the narrator (but not by Pangloss, whose stories—e.g., 221—are as devoted to prescribed statements, rigid causal sequences, system, and teleology as his more explicit "logical" arguments); this kind is respectful of facts and contexts, mindful that the world is full of discontinuities and singularities, and preferring the (correct) listing of events to their (often spurious) totalization. *Candide* pits dogmatic philosophy against circumstantial narrative and opts for the latter.

Panglossian philosophy is atemporal, acontextual, and general. What it tells is supposed to be true regardless of circumstances, and even when self-consistent, it cannot be specifically compatible with and tailored to the real world. Good narrative, in contrast, is guided by relevance. It presents spatiotemporal events related to men and women's engagement in the world. It shrinks from abstraction and thrives on concreteness. It focuses on the particular and not the general. It records what happened (and what is happening) rather than what will (supposedly) happen or what may happen. It develops in terms of an everyday practical logic and makes room for contradictions that formal logic cannot accommodate. In short, it obviates the need for metaphysical demonstrations and preachments by telling it like it is.

6... Written Narrative

Madame Bovary can be said to constitute an implicit but sustained meditation on narrative,[1] and it has often been discussed as such.[2] Gustave Flaubert's novel presents a world teeming with narratives. It abounds in characters who tell stories or, at the very least, produce narrative seeds, turn out protonarratives, create possible narrative representations. Apart from the protagonist's extravagant constructions, there are, for example, the bombastic, nefarious, and silly narratives of Homais, the foolish and tendentious narratives of Bournisien, the inane stories of Charles, the frequently efficient but wholly conventional ones of Rodolphe. But there are also Mr. Dubocage warning Léon of the dangers awaiting him (342), the irrepressible beadle in the Rouen cathedral (288–90), Mr. Guillaumin (357–58), Lestiboudois (88, 400), Hivert (102), Binet (261), and even the book lender (401).

Indeed, the characters who manifest few if any propensities for narrative, those who show little or no narratorial ambition, are quite rare: Larivière, Justin, Hippolyte, and some accessory figures. They make up a group that is practically exempt from Flaubert's irony and fulminations,[3] in contrast with the potential or actual tellers, the many budding novelists who do not escape ridicule or worse and whose products—especially those stemming from self-aggrandizement and self-advancement—

are repeatedly denounced. It is as if those who do not tell, those who reveal no particular desire or affinity for narrative, need not be treated negatively. Though their eventual lot may be sad (Flaubert ultimately tolerates no competitors), their motives and behavior do not have to be disparaged or condemned. The case of Dr. Larivière is particularly clear. This physician, who loves his art and practices it with exaltation and sagacity, tells no tales but also brooks no tales: "His gaze, more cutting than his bistouries, went down into your soul and disarticulated every lie, against all allegations and all proprieties" (377). He is a truly superior being, the only great artist in the world presented, undoubtedly greater than the other artists or artist figures portrayed: Lagardy, say, or Binet, or the Blind Man. Lagardy, the celebrated tenor, has a beautiful voice and a lot of presence but in the final analysis is nothing more than a talented ham: "More temperament than intelligence and more grandiloquence than lyricism further embellished this admirable charlatanic nature, in which there was something of the hairdresser and of the toreador"(268). Binet—who proves a weak narrator (261)—owns a lathe: he makes napkin rings as well as fake ivory pieces that bring him "one of those complete happinesses that perhaps belong only to mediocre occupations and that amuse the mind with facile difficulties and satiate it through an achievement beyond which there is no room for dreaming" (360). The Blind Man too—as we will see—is severely limited. Of course, even Larivière, for all his greatness, cannot function as the narrator's rival in the artistic domain, because he belongs to a "now extinct generation" (377).[4] The case of Justin, who is hardly ever heard, follows the same general pattern. Granted, he cries easily (147), and his romanticism may be excessive. But he is only a child; he shows true capacities for love; and — though he becomes a mere grocer's assistant — he educes real sympathy from Flaubert.[5] Finally, Hippolyte has attributes that the novelist certainly prizes: he is simpleminded, monstrous (clubfooted), and martyrized.[6] They help to explain the (relative) kindness with which he is portrayed, but they also help to indicate that simplicity, marginality, and suffering do not necessarily lead to artistic creation: Hippolyte remains Hippolyte.

The abundance of narratives and narrators criticized by Flaubert signals one of the important oppositions which — along with and perhaps more than the contrasts between Emma and Homais, the latter and Bournisien, and the heroine and her husband — govern the novel and preside over its deployment: the opposition between the activities of the creatures inhabiting the narrated world and the artistic vision of Flaubert (nothing provokes his angry verve more than Homais's artistic pretensions, 404–5) or, more specifically, the opposition between the characters' "bad narratives" and the "good narrative" that the novel evokes antiphrastically. I will attempt to sketch this "good narrative" by concentrating on Madame Bovary and her productions.

Whatever the links between Emma and the novelist, whatever the meaning one should give to the famous "Madame Bovary, c'est moi" (Madame Bovary is what I was, what I could have been? Madame Bovary is the "I" that I am not when I write? I can — I know how to — be Emma but she could not be Flaubert? I am both male and female or, rather, I am neither?), the heroine unquestionably represents the focus of the text's narrative preoccupations. True, as I have already emphasized, the novel attacks or dismisses a wide range of narrators and narrative products: gossipy anecdotes (259); political narrations

(177–78, 181–82); facile accounts relying on fate as a principle of explanation (180, 222, 244, 409); conventional stories, whether they be religious (Bournisien—382, 390–91—on the powers of God and the powers of confession), sentimental and bourgeois (Charles—235–36—envisioning Berthe's future), doxically provincial, journalistic, scientistic (Homais—150–51, 187–88, 379—on student life in Paris, the agricultural fair, the protagonist's agony), or, of course, wildly romantic (Emma); and, even more generally, untruthful narratives, whose source or motor is not so much convention as ignorance (Homais on medieval theater, 235), blindness (Homais on Léon's visits to the Bovarys, 331), vanity (the pharmacist again and the story of his success, 332), or malevolence (the pharmacist on the Blind Man, 404). But the protagonist constitutes the text's privileged opponent and target: *Madame Bovary* versus Madame Bovary.

Emma is not without intelligence; at any rate, we learn that her father thought she had "too much wit for agriculture" (39), that she "understood catechism well and . . . always answered Monsieur le Vicaire's difficult questions" (53), and that she received "little books" and "little crowns" as school prizes (38, 64). Nor is she without education (after all, she went to the Ursuline convent) or good manners: "[She] knew how to manage her household. She sent the patients the account for their visits in well-phrased letters that had no suggestion of a bill. When they had, on Sundays, some neighbor to dinner, she found a way of making a fancy dish, knew how to put pyramids of green-gages on vine leaves, served pots of preserves upside down in a plate, and, even, she spoke of buying finger bowls for the dessert" (60). She is strongly attracted by writing and buys herself "a blotting-pad, a stationery case, a penholder, and envelopes" even before she has an addressee (81). She writes Rodolphe every night and sometimes also in the middle of the day (198, 225); by means of her letters to Léon, she catches glimpses of "another man, a ghost fashioned out of her most ardent memories, her most beautiful readings, her most powerful lusts" (343); and during her agony she has a strong taste of ink in her mouth (372) and vomits "a kind of white gravel" as well as "billows of black liquids" (372, 390). She lives for narratives. She dreams of them. She dies because of them: her suicide follows her refusal of a possible and, to her, intolerable scenario in which she would confess her sins to Charles and he would forgive her (359–60). Yet the narrative production of this *femme à histoires* constitutes a total failure.

It is not only or not so much that Emma proves technically mediocre ("she began to tell him everything, hurriedly, disjointedly . . . and [was] so abundantly prodigal of parentheses that he understood nothing of it," 233), or that she gets lost in details and does not know how to carry a narrative through to an end ("She was seized with the temptation to flee with Léon, somewhere, very far away, in order to try a new destiny, but at once a vague abyss full of darkness opened within her soul," 136), or that her writing lacks distinction: the only words we know of this writing—"Do not speak of this to my husband, you know how proud he is. . . Excuse me. . . Yours obediently" (340), or else "Let no one be accused" (373)—are not exactly striking and, besides, we learn that several of her letters to Rodolphe are "technical and urgent like business notes" (242). Nor is it only that she consumes with the same eagerness Hugo, Balzac, and George Sand, *La Corbeille* and *Le Sylphe des Salons*, mawkish romances, silly keepsakes, and trivial stories about fashionable people; that she favors the gaudy, the affected, the stereotypical; that she longs to banish the monotonous without grasping that it inheres in the recurrence (84) of "endless adventures" (Flaubert, on the contrary, makes plenty of room for repetition, placing the protagonist under its sign and frequently resorting to iterative narration; he often rejects opportunities for big scenes, whether it be the death of Charles's first wife or the birth of Charles's daughter; and he relates ultimately inconsequential events: "Since the events about to be recounted, nothing in fact has changed in Yonville"; 95).[7] Nor is it either that the protagonist detests "commonplace heroes and temperate sentiments, such as there are in nature" and that she adores "stories that rush along all in a breath" (107), whereas Flaubert's text, particularly in the first five chapters, multiplies pauses, starts and restarts, changes of rhythm and direction. Or, rather, Emma's tastes—her bad taste!—like her technical weaknesses and her difficulties, simply constitute versions, symptoms, results of certain narrative conceptions and certain personal lacks.

Emma wants to be a narrative. She wants to replace existence with narrative, to discover and invent herself through narrative. Thinking that the sign can be the thing or can create it, that to tell is to take possession of, she evokes in order to own, recounts in order to receive, consumes and fabricates narratives in order to gratify the cravings of the flesh, satiate her need for money, and put an end to her passion-induced melancholy (135). As a result, she only produces—she can only produce—conventional, mercenary, and disappointing stories. They are incomplete when not deceitful ("Emma perceived [only two or three of these tableaux of Parisian life] which concealed from her all the others and represented by themselves the whole of humanity," 79) or biased or, worse, unjust ("What was it that she had done—she who was so intelligent!—to be mistaken once again? Besides, through what deplorable mania had she thus ruined her existence with continual sacrifices? . . . And for what? for what? . . . It was for him [Charles], for this creature, for this man who understood nothing, who felt nothing," 223) or deluded, not to say blind. They have no essential link with what is. Emma's desire—for the other (like any desire), for herself as other—is fashioned in terms of others, and what she considers most personal and singular turns out to be most banal.[8] The stories she imagines, the plots she accumulates, inflame her longings rather than fulfilling them, prove difficult to trade, and bring little in return (if they convince Charles, they fail to move Guillaumin, Binet, or the bankers in Rouen); and, far from providing her with a grip on life, they lead to her death.

Emma's narrative passions no doubt partly spring from the environment in which she grew up ("Accustomed to the calm aspects [of life], she turned, on the contrary, to the exciting ones," 54) and from the milieu in which she lives, from her education—"above the condition into which she was born" (442), said Marie-Antoine-Jules Sénard, who defended Flaubert and *Madame Bovary* in court—and from her readings. But these passions are also the result of more personal defects, which they intensify. Temperamentally sentimental (whence her taste, contrasting with that of the novel, for emotions and not for landscapes) as well as mercantilist ("she ha[s] to get a kind of personal profit out of things," and her narratives are tied to eroticism and commerce), practical-minded (that is, in the context of the novel, close-minded), Emma has neither discipline nor perseverance (54, 57–58, 77–78, 257). She lacks courage (59, 153, 340). She also lacks kindness and understanding: "She sometimes threw beggars all the change in her purse, though she was by no means tender nor easily open to the feelings of others" (88). And her laziness, her bad faith (153, 223, 269), her vanity (223, 265), her egoism make her incapable of "understanding what she [does] not experience and of believing anything that [does] not manifest itself in conventional forms" (62).

Madame Bovary, on the contrary, resists and subverts convention; it is (mostly) in the third person, favors the use of free indirect discourse, the mixing of the narrator's voice, language, semantic and axiological systems with those of one character or another, and offers many inside views. The good narrator—as the opposite of Emma and of other deficient tellers in the text—has an artistic attitude and knows how to overcome hamminess and bombast (see 268). He or she takes risks, is firm and constant, judicious and penetrating, generous, impartial, and precise. And good narrative proves, above all, disinterested, objective (which is, no doubt, underlined by the large number of perspectives adopted and voices used in the novel), and impersonal. It is not impersonal in the sense that the narration bears no mark of an "I"; though Flaubert never resorts to first-person singular pronouns, one can find many other first-person signs in *Madame Bovary*, from the "we" that peppers the narrative (e.g., 15, 54, 181, 333) to the present tenses and deictics relating to the time of the narrating (e.g., "But to this day, [Lestiboudois] carries on the cultivation of his tubercles, and even maintains with assurance that they grow naturally," 95) and to the passages designating texts or worlds familiar to the narrator and the narratee ("It was one of those pure feelings that do not hamper the conduct of life, that are cultivated because they are rare, and whose loss would afflict more than their possession rejoices," 134). It is impersonal, rather, in the sense that the narrative is not about the narrator's person and does not appertain to it. For in good narrative, it is not a question of creating, situating, or expressing oneself. *Who* speaks in *Madame Bovary*? whose *self*? The prominence of free indirect discourse like the diverse incarnations of Flaubert, who goes to school with Charles (15–18), attends the Yonville agricultural fair (181), and is often endowed with omniscience, make answers problematic.[9] Rather, it is a matter of saying the world. It is a question not of changing the world but of showing it, not of inventing but of discovering, not of trading (what is Flaubert's novel exchanged or exchangeable for? what is the contract underlying it? how much is it worth?) but, instead, of presenting. What is necessary is to resist cratylism (the sign is not the thing), poeticism (it does not make the thing), and commerce (it is not for sale); what is required is to distinguish between an object and its shadow and to prefer the real to the phantasmal.

The rejection of the personal and the mercenary is underlined by the switch from first- to third-person narration, from "We were in the study room" (15) to "His father, Mr. Charles-Denis-Bartholomé Bovary" (18) or, more definitively, to "He was a boy of even temperament" (22): this will not be a first-person narrative. It is also underlined by the censure of stories springing from sex/gender or linked to memory, a faculty on which Flaubert's production does not depend: "It would now be impossible for any of us to remember anything about him" (22). The novel rejects sweet and "effeminate" narratives such as the stories that Charles's mother tells her son and that are (metonymically) put together with jams and with babbling nonsense (20). The novel also rejects inflated, smug, and "virile" narratives such as those of Homais, who is well named (*homme*) and who, though undeniably verbal, uses—*pace* Naomi Schor[10]—a language full of clichés and produces narratives that are both laughable and false: he compares the agricultural fair to a scene from the *Thousand and One Nights* (188); he thinks that apricots may be the cause of Emma's fainting spells (250–51); and he believes that Léon is having an affair with Emma's maid (331). Above all, the novel rejects narratives issuing from androgynous and lascivious sources. We know that Emma admires "real" men (59) and envies their lot (113, 174, 278, 366); she wears a tortoiseshell eyeglass like a man's (31); she also dresses her hair like a man's (154), sports a man's hat (194) and men's styles (231), and likes cigarettes and pipes (200, 231, 327); after her wedding night, she acts more like the groom and Charles more like the bride (47); and later in the novel Léon becomes her mistress rather than she his (329). We also know that Emma's narrative flights exhaust her "more than great debaucheries" (344). There remains the chaste narrative—or, better, the asexual and genderless one—that *Madame Bovary* no doubt aspires to be. As for memory, it is to be noted that Charles had a very good one (21) and that the faculty, in Flaubert's text, is always mixed with sensations, desires, or dreams and always proves disordered, partial, and unreliable (e.g., 27, 47–48, 77, 128, 242).

It is their contamination by memory or by what is linked to it—the oral, the anecdotal, the eyewitness account, the personal—which ultimately undermines the interest and power of even those (truthful) narratives told by characters that the text treats with relative kindness: Rouault, for instance, or the Blind Man. No doubt Rouault is a pretty good person. But his memories are clouded by "the fumes of feasting" as well as those of emotion (48), and his letters—which recount without affectation what has happened to him—hardly go beyond the level of personal anecdotes and cackle "like a hen half hidden in a thorn of bushes" (209). The Blind Man too is not without qualities. He looks truly monstrous and appears to be feeble-minded (354), but he knows how to "*perform theatricals*" (354) and can be forgiven if he does it for gain; he gives a partial but striking summary of Emma's life ("*Often the warmth of a beautiful day / Makes a young girl dream of love,*" 371); and though he believes in Homais's promise of a miracle remedy, he refuses to be intimidated by him. Yet he stubbornly keeps on recounting to the stagecoach travelers the pharmacist's vain attempts to cure him (403): that is, he stubbornly keeps on relating his own story, and he ends up "condemned to perpetual confinement in an asylum" (404).

But is not any narrative doomed to failure or to derision, given the very nature of language (according to the text)? Flaubert's explicit statements in the novel are worth quoting: "No one, ever, can give the exact measure of his or her needs, nor of his or her conceptions, nor of his or her sorrows . . . human speech is like a cracked cauldron on which we hammer out melodies to make bears dance when we would want to move the stars" (231); and again: "Speech is a rolling-mill that always stretches feelings" (280), which recalls the "stretching of perspective that memory gives to things" (128). How would a narrator, whatever his or her attributes, talents, aspirations, and allegiance to truth, be able to show what is and to produce a "good (truthful) narrative?" Note, first, that narrative in *Madame Bovary* is autonomous in relation to language and does not need language in order to be: on their way to the Ursuline convent, Emma and her father stop at an inn where they have supper on "painted plates" representing "the story of

Mademoiselle de la Vallière" (52–53). Moreover, the impossibility signified by Flaubert's statements refers, above all, to the expression of something personal and aiming to move; it does not necessarily refer to the (detached) narration of all and any sequences of events. Finally, and most important, it is not quite *language* which is deficient but, rather, *speech* (*la parole*), that which goes from particular(s) to particular(s). Thus, good narrative may not be impossible, provided that it is not only impersonal (not expressive of *my* needs, conceptions, sorrows, feelings) and objective (transcending individual views and rhetoric) but also "silent" (not spoken, not wedded to speech, its itineraries and imperatives). In other words (recall Emma vomiting all the "ink" that she did not know how to use), good narrative, in order to be telling, must be written.

7... Narrative as Antagonist

In *Maupassant the Novelist*, Edward D. Sullivan notes that in presenting the rise of Georges Duroy, the protagonist of *Bel-Ami*,[1] from a sordid furnished apartment on the rue Boursault and a meager salary of 1,500 francs a year to a job as editor-in-chief of *La Vie Française* and a marriage with the immensely rich Suzanne Walter at the church of the Madeleine, Guy de Maupassant "skipped rapidly, too rapidly, over one phase of his career. At the end of chapter IV, in a single page of bald summary, he transforms Duroy from a fumbling apprentice into a clever, experienced reporter."[2] Duroy never wrote anything before trying his hand at journalism (12). His first article is dictated to him by his friend's wife, Madeleine Forestier (43–46). His second piece, which he composes alone, amounts to a collection of absurdities (64) and, despite revision and reworking, does not get published (67). He often fails to speak clearly (accounting for thirty-four of the sixty-six instances of stammering or stuttering in the novel)[3] and frequently finds himself at a loss for words (e.g., 14, 18, 22, 25). Yet barely two months after he starts at *La Vie Française*, he is described as "a remarkable reporter, certain of his information, crafty, swift, subtle, a real asset for the newspaper, as old Walter, who knew all about journalists, would say" (68). Duroy's subsequent career, in which he repeatedly proves to be one of the top writers of *La*

Vie Française (162) and makes himself indispensable to its boss Walter (259), is quite as impressive. He becomes "news" editor (*chef des Echos*) in less than seven months (116), political editor in less than two years (215), and editor-in-chief in just over three years.

According to Sullivan, Maupassant spends little time on a description of the newspaper world and Duroy's apprenticeship because he wants, above all, to show his protagonist succeeding through amorous adventures.[4] The point is no doubt well taken. The novelist himself made it clear, in a reply to those who criticized his text as an unfair depiction of journalism, that journalism was not what he was interested in. He used it only for the sake of convenience: "This milieu was more favorable for me than any other to show my character's stages clearly; and also . . . newspapers lead to everything, as has often been repeated."[5] More compellingly, perhaps, Maupassant's novel consistently foregrounds Duroy's success with the opposite sex and underlines its links with his journalistic and socioeconomic progress. The very first page reveals that the female customers at the restaurant he frequents—three little workers, a music teacher, and two middle-class ladies—cannot help looking at him (3). Later, Rachel, the Folies-Bergères prostitute, finds him attractive enough not to want his money (18–19). Laurine, a little girl who is very shy with men, thinks him irresistible and coins the name "Bel-Ami," which many will use when referring to him (85). Mme de Marelle takes care of him financially and provides him ready access to society or, rather (she is more of a *demi-mondaine* than a *mondaine*), to its outskirts. The widowed Madeleine Forestier marries him and makes of him an increasingly visible and dangerous journalist by writing his articles at least in part. Virginie Walter, his boss's wife, gives him power over bankers and politicians by revealing their intrigues and machinations. Finally, her daughter, Suzanne Walter, marries him after his divorce from Madeleine, thereby securing for him the job of editor-in-chief and transforming him into one of the kings of the world (361).[6]

The novel also contains indications that Bel-Ami's rapid rise is not necessarily exceptional or particularly surprising. Capable of wit (116, 142) and good at innuendo (214), shrewd, cunning and resourceful (39, 117), remarkably lucky too (thus, Forestier "saves" him just as he is about to accept a job of riding master that would mean the end of any possibility of success), Duroy is powerfully driven by desire (about half of the instances of *désir* and its derivatives in the novel—twenty-three of forty-seven, I think—pertain to him): desire for women, desire for revenge (he is an angry young man, full of rancor and spite against those above him),[7] desire for money, for power, for a name (he becomes D. de Cantel, Du Roy in two words, Du Roy de Cantel, and finally baron Du Roy de Cantel).[8] Furthermore, he is highly attractive to and highly admired by men as well as women. His army buddies have no doubt that he will succeed (39). Walter, who appreciates his slyness and intelligence and is very much an expert in these matters (116, 347), knows that he will go far (335–36) and flatly predicts that he will be a government minister one day (347). Norbert de Varenne, the poet, is kind to him and treats him like an intellectual equal (129, 314). M. de Marelle considers him most interesting and pleasant (160, 162–63); Count Vaudrec enjoys his conversation (212–13); and Jacques Rival, the famous reporter and duelist, finds his behavior during the duel with Louis Langremont entirely appropriate (158).[9]

Besides, the world inhabited by Duroy is not very difficult to conquer. Others have risen and others will rise at least in part thanks to women and/or good looks: there is Forestier and there is Jean Le Dol; there is Laroche-Mathieu; there is Rival, perhaps (238), the priest at the Trinité (256), and even the bishop of Tangiers (360). At the beginning of the novel, Forestier tells the protagonist: "You see, my boy, everything depends upon assurance here. A moderately clever man becomes a minister more easily than he becomes the head of a department" (9). Norbert de Varenne notes that among the blind the one-eyed is king (129) and insists on the spiritual mediocrity of human beings and on their profound immorality (148); Duroy himself sees everywhere around him examples of infamy (136); and the narrator repeatedly points to the baseness, cowardice, and dishonesty making up the human heart (280, 304, 359).

Still, there is some evidence, I think, that Bel-Ami's success does not simply show how certain attractive, ambitious, and moderately talented people can make it in certain circumstances. Journalism is not used merely for the sake of convenience. Duroy proves too well suited for the discursive mode it represents, a mode constituting the opponent in terms of which the novelist articulates a vision of his own activity. Part of what is at stake in the depiction of the protagonist's triumph as a writer and the description of the world in which it occurs is, I argue, the attempt by the novel at (an *ideal*) self-definition.[10]

If Maupassant disposes of Duroy's apprenticeship very quickly and does not provide many details of the actual composition or production of a newspaper, he is more eloquent about the contents of *La Vie Française* and its competitors. Forestier points out Norbert de Varenne to the protagonist very early in the novel and says: "Every story he gives us costs three hundred francs, and the longest do not run to two hundred lines" (12).

Journalistic writing is, from the outset, associated with narrative and fabulation, characterized as a commodity, and described in terms of its mediocre length (*Bel-Ami* is Maupassant's longest work, and the novelist proudly told his manservant, François Tassart: "I have finished *Bel-Ami*; I hope that it will satisfy those who were always asking me for something lengthy; for there are pages and pages, and tight ones!").[11]

The numerous other references to Duroy's and his colleagues' products emphasize the same characteristics and foreground features related to them. Journalists are "retailers of human comedy at so much a line" (25).[12] "News" items (*les Echos*), which constitute the heart of a newspaper (118), prove especially lucrative because of the disguised ads they contain (62). Like the pieces surrounding them, they are rhetorical rather than descriptive, organized in terms of an end, of a point (the question of length, again!), of their potential effect upon the reading public (46, 118, 214). Tirades substitute for ideas. Conventions and formulas count more than observation. Fictions and lies take the place of facts and life. Saint-Potin has no intention of interviewing General Li-Theng-Fao and Rajah Pali to find out what they think of English policies in the Far East: "As if I did not know it better than themselves, what they ought to think for the readers of *La Vie Française*. I've already interviewed five hundred of these Chinese, Persians, Hindus, Chilians, Japanese, and the like. They all answer the same thing, according to me. I only have to go back to my article on the last comer and to copy it word for word. What changes, of course, is their appearance, their name, their titles, their age, their retinue. Oh! about that, there must be no mistake, because I would quickly be showed up by *Le Figaro* or *Le Gaulois*" (61–62). Though she knows nothing about the subject,

Madeleine writes "Recollections of a Cavalry Man in Africa" for Bel-Ami: first, she supposes that he is conveying his impressions to a friend, which allows for remarks of all kinds; she then fabricates a short section on political geography, continues with the description of a trip to Oran, complete with Moorish, Jewish, and Spanish women (that's what the readers want!), and ends with the story of an affair between Bel-Ami and a factory worker (44–46). The protagonist, who has trouble finding ideas, follows a safe course: "He made a specialty of declamations on the decadence of morals, the abasement of characters, the weakening of patriotism, and the anemia of French honor" (162).

When Bel-Ami had proved unable to write his first article, he had said that all he needed was a little practice (40, 41). He was almost right. Journalism is easy. It takes some practice, a certain amount of shrewdness, and also the ability to copy. The *Echos* are well named. Forestier reworks pieces composed by his wife and based on outlines that Walter and his "gang" provide (119). Similarly, Bel-Ami functions as a mouthpiece (267) and secretary who mostly writes whatever is dictated to him (214, 268, 307), and if a good article on Morocco is needed, he produces one in forty-five minutes by patching up "Recollections of a Cavalry Man in Africa" (260–61). Nor is copying confined to *La Vie Française*; its competitors look to it for much of their information (267) and lift entire passages from it (215).

In its affinity for repetition, its dependence on formula, fiction, and falsehood, its manipulative concerns, its scantiness, its commercial nature, journalistic writing constitutes an important manifestation of the novelist's ultimate enemy: narrative (and the novel based on narrative). Maupassant frequently and explicitly refers to narrative in *Bel-Ami* (there are at least twenty-five occurrences of the verb *raconter*, "to recount," and at least as many instances of related terms and expressions: *conter, conteur, conte, histoire, réciter, récit,* and so on).[13] He describes it in the terms used to describe journalistic writing and elaborates his negative critique. Etymologically, of course, *récit* is linked to repetition and so is *raconter*. The *récit* is a re-citing, a re-signaling, a re-starting, and *raconter* means to give a second account, to re-account. In the novel, too, narrative services the already said and done, the hackneyed, the rehearsed. To continue the tale begun by Madeleine Forestier, Duroy accumulates bits and pieces from *feuilleton* novels, extravagant adventures, and bombastic descriptions (64). To convince her mother that she will marry Duroy and no one else, Suzanne recites to her a carefully prepared little story (343). Narrative is based on rumor and gossip, chitchat and fantasy, counterfeiting and alteration; it is linked to problematic memory ("He tried to seize again bits of reminiscences and to fix them: they escaped him as fast as he took hold of them," 62), exchange ("She started to question him as a priest would have done in the confessional, asking precise questions that reminded him of details forgotten, characters encountered, faces merely glimpsed," 44), and desire ("He imagined a magnificent adventure of love which brought him, all at once, to the fulfillment of his hopes," 39). Relying on the facilities of the ready-made, the imperatives of the marketplace, the magnet of the possible, narrative expresses not the past but at best its (imperfect) recollection, not the present but its (distorted) retailing, not the future but its (often deluded) expectation. It supplies a simulacrum of reality, and though it sometimes may prove interesting, it always does prove interested. The determination to reach a certain goal, to seduce and subjugate, animates it: "He invented a touching story" (99); "He gave a dramatic account" (159). Its value is tied to circumstance: "He encouraged her to talk nonsense, to chatter, to recount all these childish things, all these tender trifles that lovers spout. This babble, which he found delightful in the mouth of Mme de Marelle, would have exasperated him in that of Mme Walter" (285). Driven by the necessity to make a point, it posits an origin ("I have to start with my departure," 36; "I would like to recount my trip from the beginning," 43) and is magnetized by an end; in order to bridge them in an acceptable and telling way, it proffers appearance, sacrifices fact, and misses life, the specificity, unpredictability, and irreducibility of being and truth (see 159, 189, 242, 252).

Now Georges Duroy is an exemplary narrative animal and is portrayed as such from the beginning: "Tall, well-built, blond—a slightly reddish chestnut blond—with a twisted-up moustache that seemed to sparkle on his lip, light blue eyes with very small pupils, hair naturally curling and parted in the middle, he looked very much like the rascal of popular novels" (4). His consciousness is shaped by the stories he heard in the army (39), and as he gets to know the secrets of the rich of this world, he becomes a kind of "almanac of Parisian celebrities and scandals" (135). Duroy has several clearly positive attributes: good looks, a charming voice (32, 192), a real feeling for nature (162, 200, 205), a certain amount of filial devotion (209, 361). Furthermore, his sensuality, his ambition, his easy cynicism, even his scorn for women are by no means assessed negatively. In fact, they make him rather similar to Maupassant himself.[14] Perhaps only insofar as he exemplifies "narrative man" does he provoke his creator's unambiguous censure.

Like narrative, Duroy thrives on appearance and lives by repetition. His stammers and stutters prove symptomatic, and so does his habit of talking to himself aloud (e.g., 6, 7, 21). More decisively, he is tributary to the positive images conveyed to him by a series of mirrors (20, 21, 34). His career consists in pursuing and conforming to these images: "Suddenly, he saw in front of him a gentleman in full dress who was looking at him . . . a burst of joy gave him a start . . . he had not even recognized himself: he had taken himself for someone else, for a man of the world. . . . Then he studied himself as actors do to study their roles" (20–21); and his success derives in part from his ability to dismiss the negative or misleading reflections he is the only one to see (113, 151).[15] Seeking to become the copy of a copy, mimicking what this one says (33) and that one does (71), incapable of understanding that which departs from a well-worn pattern—he finds Mme Walter intolerable because she acts like a teenager (273–74)—Duroy is a mere reproduction. His desires are, of course, founded on imitation[16]—he wants to be like Forestier, then like Laroche-Mathieu, then like Walter—and even his triumphs with women are touched by repetition: "Words of love . . . are always the same" (285). Rachel is just a prostitute; he substitutes for Madeleine's first husband (and his fellow journalists call him Forestier); he functions as another M. de Marelle (162, 185); he takes the place of Walter; and in the case of Suzanne, he has to displace the Marquis de Cazolles. Only with Laurine is he unequivocally "first"; but she is only a child, and besides, he cannot hold on to her.

Like narrative too, Duroy views life in terms of plot. He is obsessed with ends ("His native Norman conscience . . . had become a kind of trick box in which one could find something of everything. But the desire to succeed reigned sovereign in it," 39) and given to measuring how far he stands from his beginnings ("I have to write dad tomorrow. If he saw me, tonight, in the house I am going to, wouldn't the old man be amazed," 122; "He was becoming one of the masters of the earth, he, he, the son of two poor peasants from Canteleu," 361). He stages over and over again what he would like to see occur (esp. 38–39, 82–83, 155–56) and retells to his advantage what has already happened (102–3, 159, 299). Indeed, Duroy's ascent parallels his progressive understanding of plot. In the opening scenes of the novel, he is capable only of vague dreams about amorous exploits and financial triumphs (38–39); he does not know how to begin (see 36, 41, 64), how to defer, how to construct (36, 62). Slowly, he learns the formulas governing plot—"Many had paid their debts (an honorable action) without its ever being guessed where the necessary money had come from (a very fishy mystery)" (136)—and his projects gain in complexity and precision, though they still frequently go awry (107, 108–9). By the second half of the novel, he has acquired all the tools necessary to engineer a complicated and winning intrigue (169, 177–78, 310). Victory then proves easy.

Easy and illusory. If Maupassant is thought to have skipped too rapidly over Duroy's metamorphosis into a first-rate reporter, he is also thought to have granted too much time to a scene (130–34) in which Norbert de Varenne explains to the protagonist that successes do not matter and do not last, that goals are achieved merely in a superficial manner, and that the only reality and end is death: "To breathe, sleep, drink, eat, work, dream, everything that we do is to die. To live, ultimately, is to die! . . . Oh! you will realize that! . . . What do you expect? Love? A few more kisses and you will be impotent. And then what? Money? To do what? To pay women? Some fun that will be! To eat a lot, become obese, and scream for entire nights under the bites of gout? And then what else? Glory?

What use is that when you can no longer get it in the form of love? And then what? Always death at the end" (131).[17] The length of the scene has been and can be explained by Maupassant's own obsession with death.[18] Yet, it seems to me that it is also justified textually. It announces the agony and end of Charles Forestier and the fear that they arouse in the protagonist (168, 176–77). It further announces Duroy's terror on the eve of his duel (150–53). More crucially, it undermines—indeed negates—all his victories. Finally, it makes clear that narrative ends, and everything they support or imply, are fake.

Not for Maupassant the totalizing conclusion, the accidents and complications setting up one privileged moment, the conventional, falsely pretty, and falsely graceful poses occasioned by transaction and point. He criticizes them in *Bel-Ami* (206, 240, 340, 342), and like many realists and naturalists, he attacks them frequently in other texts ("One must break the chains of tradition, shatter the molds of imitation, empty the phials labeled with poetic elixir, and venture, innovate, find, create"; "The novelist must not plead, or chatter, or explain. Only facts and characters must speak").[19] Adventure novels—by Mlle de Scudéry, Eugène Sue, Frédéric Soulié, Alexandre Dumas—are not "real." Neither are the "preachy" novels—of Jean-Jacques Rousseau, George Sand—that serve some general idea or system, or "arty" ones emphasizing the wit and talent of their author.[20] Not for Maupassant narrative and the novel wedded to narrative. In October 1891 he would even write: "I have thought it over and I am absolutely determined not to do stories or novellas anymore. It is hackneyed, worn out, ridiculous. Besides, I have done too many of them. I want to work only on my novels and not divert my mind with little stories away from the only work which fascinates me."[21]

The techniques at work in *Bel-Ami*, the objects and events it celebrates, the very nature of the world and life it presents underline Maupassant's desire to distance himself from narrative or at least from those aspects of it that he characterizes negatively. Most obvious, perhaps, is the refusal to end. Duroy marries Suzanne Walter. The ultimate goal has seemingly been reached. But the last few pages of the novel insist on a series of beginnings. Madeleine, for example, is now with Jean Le Dol, a good-looking and intelligent young man who writes articles very similar to those of the protagonist: "Whence I concluded," says Norbert de Varenne, "that she loved beginners and would love them eternally" (357). As for Duroy, he sees the Parliament House as he comes out of the Madeleine and thinks of the political career ahead of him (363). He also sees Mme de Marelle, whom he had left three months earlier (362). Their affair is not over, and the last image of the novel is that of the young woman adjusting her hair after she gets out of bed (363). Duroy seems condemned not to know the end. He is an *arriviste* and will continue indefinitely to arrive.

Other technical features are to be noted: the beginning as continuation (when he meets Forestier, Duroy has been in Paris for a few months, working in a railroad company and, night after night, taking walks along the boulevards); the adherence to chronological order, to the "natural" order of occurrence of events; the protagonist's lack of introspection (there is no going over what has occurred); the use of internal focalization and the prominence of dialogue (the text presents what happens directly as it happens or as it is perceived, without analysis, arrangement, repetition); the heterodiegetic narration, the relative covertness of narratee and narrator, and the impassiveness of the latter (there is no retelling, no explicit desire on the part of a teller to recount a series of events, no transaction with a narratee, no pleading, no commentary, no lesson);²² and even the stylistic device whereby event participants are initially unspecified ("It would pass near them, this train," 38; "And he saw them too, the man and the woman . . . eating their soup in little gulps," 122; "George knew it well, this vaulted room," 237), as if the text did not have to follow the imperatives of communication.

At several points, Maupassant's text indicates more forcefully and positively its commitments and values: presentation rather than explanation, truth rather than convention, what *is* rather than what should be. Duroy, for instance, finds it surprising that M. de Marelle chose Clotilde for a wife: "What whimsical being could have arranged the coupling of this old man and this madcap woman? What reasoning made this inspector marry that undergraduate? A mystery! Who knows? Love, perhaps?" (160–61) Madeleine is shocked by Duroy's parents: "She was not unaware that she was going to visit peasants. . . . Had she seen them from afar as more poetic? No, but as more literary perhaps, more noble, more affectionate, more decorative. Yet she did not want them to be genteel like those in novels" (206). In other passages the impenetrable is given as impenetrable, the unknowable remains unknowable, the secret preserves its secrecy (see 92–93, 295–96). Twice, a "real" work of art is presented. Unpredictable, irreducible, instead of calling for analysis or commentary, it invites silence. The first is a fencing match: "They lunged and recovered themselves with supple elegance, with measured vigor, with such assurance in their strength, such correctness in their demeanor, such measure in their performance that the ignorant crowd was astonished and charmed. . . . The public felt that it was looking at a beautiful and rare thing, that two great artists at their trade were showing it the very best that one could see. . . . No one spoke anymore" (241). The second is a painting, *Jesus Walking on the Waves* by Karl Marcowitch: "It was indeed the powerful and unexpected work of a master. . . . People who looked at such a thing at first remained silent" (312). By undermining artificial closure, avoiding repetition, eschewing explanation, maintaining an impassive stance, and criticizing the conventional orderings and developments of narrative, Maupassant's text aspires to equal these two works and to define itself as *novel*.

Of course, this characterization is an *idealized* one. Chronology, for example, is not always adhered to in *Bel-Ami* (see 272, 303–6, 344ff.). Signs of the narrator are not difficult to find (14–15, 164, 206); analysis and commentary have not disappeared (39, 203, 273); and the narratee is often invited to share a given vision (37, 48, 266). The text, it could be argued, presents a story of ascent and develops it conventionally in terms of a protagonist's multiple desires and successive triumphs. It has the episodic quality of an adventure novel, and rather than constituting a disinterested, open realm, it institutes a series of moments, stories, points.[23] Perhaps the novel as envisioned in *Bel-Ami*—a novel presenting situations and events without succumbing to traditional story requirements, a novel narrating without recourse to "narrative," without narrating, as it were—is impossible. This impossibility, the subject of Maupassant's longer fictions,[24] may haunt every attempt to write a "real" novel. It is an impossibility that any such attempt may have to deny and may be forced to confirm.

8... Nausea and Narrative

The protagonist of Jean-Paul Sartre's *La Nausée*, who finds it difficult to remember his own past, has settled in Bouville after much traveling and many adventures, to complete a biography of Monsieur de Rollebon.[1] Antoine Roquentin is not a professional historian and has not produced other historical work, except perhaps for a few articles (247–48). He started his book project at least a decade earlier but, having dropped it for half a dozen years, still has much of his subject's life to cover (27–28). He retains few, if any, illusions about the value of history (87, 104) and does not seem to believe that knowledge of the past helps to understand the present: "They explain the new by the old—and the old, they have explained it by events that are older still, like those historians who make of Lenin a Russian Robespierre and of Robespierre a French Cromwell: in the final analysis, they have never understood anything at all" (102). Indeed, he writes simply for the sake of writing (27, 166), or so he thinks and says. At the beginning of the novel, Roquentin feels that "something has happened" (15). He is given to fits of nausea that he cannot comprehend, and the world around him—tobacco packs, door handles, stones, pipes and forks, faces and hands—appears to be different. He decides to investigate the meaning of this difference: "The best thing would be to write down the events from day to day. Keep a diary to see clearly. Let none of the nuances or small facts escape, even if they look like nothing, and, above all, classify them. I must say how I see this table, the street, the people, my pack of tobacco, since it is this which has changed. I must determine exactly the extent and nature of this change" (11).

Like things in general, Roquentin's biographical project is not going well. It is not that he lacks narrative ability: as far as telling a good story is concerned, he "fears no one except ship officers and professionals" (53). Nor is it that he lacks intelligence—he clearly does not—or psychological acumen. True, he has no taste for psychologizing, and when it comes to himself, he wants "no secrets or soul-states, nothing ineffable, [being] neither a virgin nor a priest to play with the inner life" (23). But the historian's trade hardly relies on psychology: "In our work, we have to do only with sentiments in the whole to which one gives generic names such as Ambition or Interest" (15). Neither is it that he feels too distant from his subject, too different from Monsieur de Rollebon. Though Rollebon has lost much of his glamour, Roquentin still shows a lot of affection for him. Besides, the two men have the same initials (Rollebon's first name was Adhémar); both are ugly but with nice hair; both keep a diary; both have led an adventurous life; and Rollebon looks like a *Roque*fort cheese and marries a lady of *Roque*laure (24).

Finally, it is not that Roquentin lacks documentation. He sometimes does, of course—what, for example, could Rollebon have been doing in the Ukraine in August 1804? (87)—but sometimes, on the contrary, "letters, fragments of memoirs, secret reports, police records, [there are] almost too many of them. What is lacking in all this testimony is firmness and consistency. They do not contradict one another, no, but neither do they agree with one another; they do not seem to be about the same person" (27). Roquentin is beginning to think that "nothing can ever be proved. [Mine] are honest hypotheses which take the facts into account: but I sense so well that they come from me, that they are very simply a way of unifying my knowledge. Not a glimmer comes from Rollebon's side. Slow, lazy, sulky, the facts adapt themselves to the rigor of the order I want to give them but it remains outside of them. I have the feeling of doing a work of pure imagination. Besides, I am sure that the characters in a novel would have a more genuine appearance, or, at any rate, would be more pleasant" (28).

Undoubtedly, Roquentin's feeling has something to do with the fact that for him the lifelike, the plausible, *le vraisemblable* (and, consequently, realist or historical narrative) is coming unglued: "I marvel at these young people: drinking their coffee, they tell clear, plausible stories. . . . When you live alone . . . the plausible disappears" (19–20). Now as the epigraph to *La Nausée* indicates—"He is a guy without collective importance. He is just an individual"—Roquentin represents *l'homme seul*. He lives alone, hardly ever speaks to anyone, gets nothing and gives nothing. He has no boss, no job, no wife, no children; he does not vote; he barely pays taxes (19, 125, 150). And he has no difficulty seeing the plausible for what it is: plausible.

Something else too is coming unglued. Roquentin, who has always thought that he had had many adventures, comes to feel that he never had any: "Things have happened to me, events, incidents, anything you like. But not adventures" (59). Adventures take place in books, not in life; they occur in narrative, not in the world. They are narrative—"for the most banal event to become an adventure, it is necessary and sufficient to start *recounting* it" (61)—and they do not *exist*. Of course, what is told about in books can and does happen in life—"the proof is that people talk about true stories" (39)—but not in the same way. This has nothing to do with the nature of the events, their quality, their content; it has to do with the form they constitute, the way that they are linked together. It has to do with the difference between life and narrative, and "one must choose: live or tell" (62).

In life, time is not a bounded and ordered sequence of signifying moments. Nothing ever happens. Nothing is essential: "The scenery changes, people come in and go out, that's all. There are never any beginnings. Days are tacked on to days without rhyme or reason; it is an interminable and monotonous addition.... Neither is there any end.... And then everything looks alike: Shanghai, Moscow, Algiers.... Monday, Tuesday, Wednesday. April, May, June. 1924, 1925, 1926" (62–63). Roquentin, who lives *in* time, does not live in time (and his keeping a diary, like his knowing the tram schedule and his frequenting the "Railwaymen's Rendezvous," constitute vain attempts to keep time). In life, there is no meaningful deployment of time or space, no passage from one homogeneity to another through heterogeneity, no necessary link between one event and the next. That's life. But with narrative, everything is different because events are viewed and told in terms of their end, an end which is there at the beginning (and even before the beginning) and which gives the beginning the force of a beginning: "events happen one way and we tell about them in the opposite way. You seem to start at the beginning. ... And in reality you have started at the end. ... And the story goes on in reverse: instants have stopped piling themselves haphazardly one on top of the other; they are snapped up by the end of the story which attracts them, and each one of them in turn attracts the instant which precedes it" (63).[2] With narrative, something begins and does so in order to end. Something happens. Something is going to end. Something ends. Everything counts and has a place, even (as in realist narrative with its reality effects) that which is given as superfluous. Everything is oriented, meaningful, irreplaceable. Everything is out of this world. What happens with adventure—with life as told, with my life as I tell it (to myself)—is that *"I am me and I am here"* (82), in time, in a sequence of indispensable moments indispensably linked together: "I think this is what happens: you suddenly feel that time is passing, that each instant leads to another instant, this one to another one, and so on; that each instant is annihilated, and that it is not possible to hold it back, etc. . . . If I remember well, they call that the irreversibility of time. The feeling of adventure would simply be that of the irreversibility of time. . . . There are moments when you have the impression that you can do what you want, go forward or backward, that it has no importance; and then others when you might say that the links have been tightened and, in these cases, it is a question of not missing your turn because you could never start again" (85–86). Narrative makes (the most of) time. It makes it feel irreversible, precious, rigorous, necessary, and in doing so, it makes real instants imaginary and transforms facts into fiction.[3]

Now biography too is narrative. It too is fictional if only because of its narrative configuration. History is just a story, and not surprisingly, Roquentin abandons his project. If he could not save his own past—"I can search the past all I want, I only find bits of images and I am not quite sure what they represent, nor whether they are memories or fictions" (53)—surely he cannot save someone else's (136). He was merely having a dream, and Rollebon was his partner in it; he provided the raw material—*existence*—and Rollebon furnished the design; he was only a means of making Rollebon live, and Rollebon was his reason for living: "He had delivered me from myself" (140). Not surprisingly either, Roquentin decides to write fiction.

In the first place, there is not much else for him to do. Roquentin refuses (or is forced to refuse) many other stories, many other *grands récits* (to speak like Jean-François Lyotard), many other myths and constructs by which human beings fashion and interpret their lives. He rejects (or is forced to reject) many ways of acting in bad faith and trying not to face the absurdity of existence: adventures and traveling and history, of course, but also knowledge (even before reaching his conclusions about history, Roquentin thinks that the Self-Taught Man is an imbecile, and early in the novel he is repulsed by a piece of paper referring to "The White Owl," the owl of wisdom); power and money (the bourgeois of Bouville are bastards); the consolations of reminiscence (the past is dead), psychology ("neither a virgin nor a priest"), and nature (it is repugnant); action (219, 241: to do what and for what?); sex (19, 88: it does not exactly thrill him); love (Roquentin and Anny have nothing to say to each other); friendship (Roquentin and the Self-Taught Man have nothing to say to each other); humanism (no comment!); and even suicide (it is not—181—much of a solution).[4]

Furthermore, Roquentin is surrounded by tired languages that exasperate and disgust him. Every word he reads or hears is already overused; symptomatically, "The White Owl" is a dictation (24). Every word is limp, slack, tarnished. He cannot stand the utterances of the Self-Taught Man—"Is it my fault if, in everything he tells me, I recognize in passing the borrowing, the quotation?" (165)—any more than he can stand the utterances of the young lovers at the Maison Bottanet or those of the couple in the Bouville museum. He is sorry that Rollebon's letters are so stiff and would rather think that the Marquis did not write them himself but "had them composed by the public scribe" (88). He despises populist works[5] and Femina prizes, "psychology as they manufacture it in novels" (122), Maurice Barrès and Paul Bourget, Henry Bordeaux and Pierre Benoit, and, above all perhaps, Balzac and *Eugénie Grandet*, which he does not have "the courage to begin from the beginning" (49), which he takes along with him one Sunday because "after all, you have to do something" (72), and which gives him little if any pleasure. Everything that he reads is flabby and lusterless. He needs to read something new, hard, brilliant. He might as well write it!

Roquentin, for some time, has been attracted by writing. One of his first reactions to nausea is to keep a diary, and he finds more and more refuge in the space it offers him. After his epiphany in the public garden ("And I—soft, languid, obscene, digesting, tossing about dismal thoughts—*I, too, was superfluous*," 181), he states: "I had learned all I could know about existence. I left, I went back to the hotel, and I wrote" (190). Similarly, as he gets ready to say a final goodbye to Bouville, he notes: "The truth is that I can't let go of my pen; I think I am going to 'have the Nausea' and I feel as though I'm delaying it by writing. So I write whatever comes into my mind" (241). Besides, well before abandoning his biographical project he had begun to lose interest in Rollebon: "Now, the man . . . the man is beginning to bore me. It is the book that attracts me; more and more, I feel the need to write it" (27). He even had the feeling of writing fiction (28), and slowly, the temptation of the novel becomes more powerful: "I should, rather, be writing a novel on the Marquis de Rollebon . . . after all, what prevents me from writing a novel about his life?" (88).

There is also "the old ragtime with a vocal refrain" (38) that Roquentin likes to listen to: "Some of These Days." It brings him a strange happiness and even makes his nausea disappear. In every respect, it is the opposite of existence. Dry, hard, compact, rhythmical, invulnerable, necessary, it carries its own death within itself "like an internal necessity" (188); it has its own time which transcends time; it is "completely self-absorbed" (243); it *is*. At the end of the novel, Roquentin sits, one last time, at the Railwaymen's Rendezvous where he listens, one last time, to his favorite song. It seems to him that the composer and the singer have managed to save themselves, to justify their existence, and he decides to save himself by writing a book, a story, a novel. Of course, it would not be a realist novel like *Eugénie Grandet*, with its conventionality and its pretense of describing reality. For the protagonist, narrative remains external to existence. Representing the real is not apprehending it. The map is not the territory, and the word is not the thing.[6] Nor would it be a humanistic novel, written for the edification of others and in communion with them. Roquentin, the *homme seul*, has little aptitude for dialogue. He fails to see the attraction of "people . . . thinking the same things all together" (21) and does not "want to be integrated" (167). Rather, it would constitute "another kind of book . . . a story that could never happen, for instance . . . beautiful and hard as steel" (247). Instead of claiming to designate and re-present that which exists, it would present that which does not exist and designate itself; instead of signaling an involvement with others, it would simply be.

But the success of Roquentin's enterprise (with the fetishization of art that it entails and the view of "good narrative" as pure fiction that it promotes) is problematic. To begin with, *La Nausée* repeatedly parodies *A la recherche du temps perdu*, and it would be odd for Sartre's novel to reach the same conclusion as Proust's and to consider art as the way to salvation.[7] Moreover, during his visit to the Bouville museum, the protagonist had severely criticized Parrottin, who led his listeners along the most perilous paths, made them reject the most sacred values, went so far that they could barely follow him. Yet "one more step and, suddenly, everything was reestablished, marvelously founded on solid reasons, as in the old days" (126). Roquentin's redemption through art would make of him (of Sartre too!) a Parrottin. No wonder that the last pages of his diary are so hesitant, multiplying conditionals and signs of indecision: "Couldn't I try . . . couldn't I . . . I don't know . . . I don't dare make a decision . . . perhaps . . . perhaps . . . perhaps" (247–48). Maybe art cannot save us from existence, and maybe the end of the novel represents still another attempt that is doomed to failure, another myth or construct to be deconstructed. Indeed, art did not save Anny, who knew how to make the most of time (86) and dreamed of transforming the situations in her life into perfect moments. But in life there are no perfect moments, any more than there are adventures (201). Anny was an artist, but she has given up on art as a way of realizing her ambition: "Paintings, statues, they're useless: they're lovely *facing* me. Music . . . [As for theater] I was in the dust, in the draft, under the raw lights, between cardboard sets. . . . The essential thing, for all of us, was the black pit just in front of us, in the bottom of which there were people we did not see; obviously we were presenting them with a perfect moment. But, you know, they did not live in it: it unfolded in front of them. And we, the actors, do you think we lived inside it? In the end, it was not anywhere, not on either side of the footlights; it did not exist" (212–13). Finally, there is the Editor's Note preceding Roquentin's diary. From the chronological point of view, it comes at the end. It also proves to be redundant (most of the information it provides is provided again by Roquentin). Besides, what has happened to Roquentin if the notebooks we read "were *found* among his papers" (9)?[8] If he has no collective importance—if he did not become a novelist, say—why publish them? and if he did, why not mention it? Instead of illuminating the protagonist's fate, the note proves ambiguous; instead of confirming the well-foundedness of his artistic project, the note puts it into question.

If salvation through art may well be a mirage, so may the kind of narrative envisaged by Roquentin. The song that he likes so much, with its promising title and its magical (English) language, functions in an equivocal manner. According to the protagonist, it is strictly concerned with itself, asking for nothing, addressing no one, referring to no existent. Except that this is not quite the case. "Some of these days / You'll miss me honey" (39). The words carry a lesson for Roquentin (do not neglect me or you will be sorry) and, at the same time, express what he wants to be: irreplaceable, necessary. The other two popular songs mentioned in the novel are no less suggestive in context. From "The Man I Love" (is this the man that Roquentin longs to be?), we get: "When the [yel]low moon begins to beam / Every night I dream a little dream" (146); and it is in connection with a dance hall called the Blue Grotto that the protagonist evokes "Blue Sky" [sic](62).[9] Jazz pieces may refer and address after all. In any case, their world is not free of all and any links with ours.

In a similar way, Roquentin's spiteful interest in *Eugénie Grandet* can be interpreted as an attack on the falseness of realism and the bankruptcy of its claims to represent existence. Yet Sartre could have picked a different Balzacian work, and it is not difficult to argue that Eugénie fascinates and disgusts Antoine as mirrors do (31–33). Granted, the contrast between Balzac's work and *La Nausée* is, in a sense, very clear: third person, first person; omniscience, nonomniscience; in the family, out of it; memory, amnesia; nature adored, nature abhorred; private garden, public garden, and so on. But in another sense the two works are very much alike. They describe the shabby hell of the provinces. They function under the sign of melancholy (*La Nausée* was to be entitled *Melancholia*) and monotony. In Bouville, nothing happens, according to Roquentin. In Saumur, years pass and do not always make a difference: at the end, Eugénie is as pure as in the beginning. The two worlds are steeped in a time which changes very few things. Like Rollebon, that other (of) Roquentin, Eugénie has a pockmarked face; like Roquentin, she is raped by the real; and if the young man is a "feminine masculine," invaded by sweetness, softness, wetness, viscousness, the young woman is a "masculine feminine": "She had an enormous head, the masculine yet delicate brow of the Jupiter of Phidias."[10] Perhaps Roquentin sees himself in Eugénie and sees his world in hers. Perhaps, if realism fails, it does not fail entirely.

But there is more. Even as Roquentin envisions a story thoroughly cleansed of existence, he suggests that his projected book will not be quite existence-free: "Another kind of book. I don't quite know which—but one would have to guess, behind the printed words, behind the pages, at something [*only something!*] which would not exist, which would be above existence" (247). And there is more still. According to Roquentin, it would not be a matter of being saved by the very activity of writing: "Naturally, at first it would only be boring and tiring work, it would not stop me from existing or from feeling that I exist" (248). And it would not be a matter of having written, of being written—neither "I write therefore I am" nor "I have written therefore I am." There is nothing left of Rollebon in his works (138–39), nothing left of Anny in her letters (94–95), nothing left of Roquentin in the words he has just put down on paper (136–37). Finally, it would not simply (or mainly) be a matter of having created something beautiful or *essential* but also a matter of being read: "A book. A novel. And there'd be people who'd read this book and say: 'It's Antoine Roquentin who wrote it, he was a red-headed guy who hung around cafés,' and they would think about my life as I think about that of the *Négresse*: as something precious and half legendary" (248). All things considered, Roquentin would be saved by others!

Perhaps, just as human beings cannot avoid narrative—"a man is always a teller of tales; he lives surrounded by his stories and the stories of others; he sees everything that happens to him through them" (61–62)—narrative cannot avoid existence and forget others. Perhaps a narrator's task is not so much to capture and reproduce reality as, rather, to give it shape; not only to discover and represent it but also, and simultaneously, to invent and transform it. Narrative may be both a partial exposition of and a temporary imposition on the world. It does not "write down events"; it gives them a meaning and signals a commitment to that meaning. Perhaps it is not quite a matter of choosing between living and telling but of choosing between one telling and another, of deciding what, how, and why to tell. After Roquentin sketches how the tired body of a "Jew with charcoal eyebrows" (245) gave birth to "Some of These Days" in the burning New York heat, he adds: "That's the way it happened. That way or another way, it makes little difference. That is how it was born" (245).[11] Perhaps one should allow for uncertainty and ignorance (renounce "saying it all" or "proving it once and for all"), explicitly blend documentation and imagination, and compose the best (the tightest!) narrative for a given set of actions and reactions, facts and feelings, a narrative which, instead of reassuring and blinding by passing off platitudes and prejudices as experience and truth (100), would "make people ashamed of their existence" (247). The work projected by Roquentin at the end of the novel may paradoxically signal the possibility of his return to history, society, the world. Perhaps: *La Nausée* does not dispense certainty.[12]

9... How to Redo Things with Words

Among many other things, Claude Simon's *La Route des Flandres* develops an attempt at solving a riddle.[1] The novel's Oedipal subtext proves insistent.[2] Georges, the protagonist, is a stranger of mixed origins (aristocrats and peasants), cut off from irretrievable ends (like all animate creatures, he cannot know his own death). Georges has been living through a series of disasters—the French collapse of 1940; a prison camp; an affair with Corinne, his captain's widow — surrounded by strangers and singular beings, by sexual transgressors and hybrid monsters, a modern horseman brandishing a sword, sphinxes, soldiers who have lost their mounts, the lower part of their bodies. His father is pachyderm-like and deformed; his captain and distant cousin has something Arabian about him and a name that causes problems: "Reishak good God [not Reixach] haven't you gotten that yet: shak the x like ess, aitch-sh and the ch at the end like k" (46); Corinne is said to be foreign to the entire human species (140); and his companions in war and defeat are crippled peasants, Jews like Blum (his frighteningly thin alter ego), Spaniards or Italians like Iglesia (whose face—37—resembles an Indian death mask), and artificial products from Malta or Algeria, with guttural names: Ahmed ben Abdahahla, or Bouhabda, or Abderhamane. Georges's quest involves a rejection of his father, an *agrégé* whose faith in the power of words seems unshakable and whose devotion to them exasperates the protagonist: "I really don't feel like aligning still more words and words and still more words. You too, in the end, don't you get sick of it. . . . Of speeches. Of engaging in . . ."(36). Georges also repudiates another father figure, Captain de Reixach, by failing to return to the scene of his death: "I proposed going back, to see whether he was dead or not. . . . After all even like that at point-blank range this guy might have missed him, might have only wounded him or only killed his horse since the horse fell when we saw him draw his saber . . . then I stopped talking realizing that I was wasting my time" (46–47). In fact, the ostensible question Georges tries to answer, even seducing Corinne in his struggle to get at the truth, is whether de Reixach allowed himself to be killed by the enemy and whether this possible suicide was motivated by his wife's possible infidelities. If the captain knowingly took his men into an ambush, or even if he rode slowly in order to rest his beloved horse instead of trying to escape at full speed (311–12), then he should provoke not guilt and remorse but, rather, anger and resentment.

But perhaps Georges is focusing on the wrong elements. For instance, sleeping with Corinne may contribute nothing to his understanding of de Reixach or of anyone or anything else: "What had I looked for in her hoped for pursued even upon her body in her body words sounds as crazy as he is with his illusory sheets of paper blackened with scrawls" (274). Besides, there is another enigma, other questions have to be answered. How could an entire regiment dissolve and disappear? And what is the relation between de Reixach's life and death and this disappearance? And is there any meaningful parallel between his possible suicide and that of his ancestor? Are we forced to repeat the same old gestures and play the same old roles? And how is it that Georges survived? What is the meaning of his experience? And is it better to be alive than dead? and what is death?

The nature of the riddle to be solved is uncertain. The question "what to know" (306) admits of no easy answer. Even if it did, another question, "how to know"—which constitutes an ever more urgent leitmotif in the novel (e.g., 85, 201, 295, 296, 301)—would pose still greater difficulties. To reconstruct a situation, to establish the meaning of a series of events, the causes and consequences of a state of affairs, the significance of a given moment or experience is, to say the least, problematic—not only or not so much because there seems to be no possibility in *La Route des Flandres* of full original presence (consciousness is always already memory, distance; events are always already being refashioned in terms of various interests and conventions)[3] and no possibility of total vision (313, 314) but also because the tools of reconstruction and reinscription, the instruments of representation (I mean language and narrative or history) appear inadequate.

Claude Simon has often commented on this inadequacy. In his (written) interview with Ludovic Janvier, for example, he states:

> It seems to me that if one reflects upon everything that separates and differentiates the "real" object or event from the written object or event, because (1) of the imperfections of our perceptual faculties; (2) of the imperfections of our memory; (3) of the choice, voluntary or not, of certain of its characteristics at the expense of others which are rejected or passed over in silence; (4) of the

very nature of writing, which unfolds in a duration and is therefore obliged to say successively what is, very often, perceived simultaneously (whence too the obligation to choose a certain order, which is also fatally arbitrary and subjective); (5) of the formal necessities and constraints of writing (syntax, composition, rhythm, sounds); (6) of the dynamics of the latter (we are governed by our language at least as much as we govern it) . . . well, if one is the least bit willing to make an effort to consider this bewildering series of deformations, it then becomes very obvious that writing cannot pretend to "redouble" the story already lived, nor to "save" it, nor to "give it a limit," but to *tell* a story which, once again, maintains with the story "already lived" only the very relative connections of the painted apple with the "real" apple.[4]

In *La Route des Flandres*, this deficiency is repeatedly emphasized. Many of the linguistic elaborations of many of the characters seem empty of reality: instead of exploring and espousing it, they remain singularly untouched by it. Georges's father, in particular, surrounds himself with graphic signs that are radically separated from existence, elegantly insignificant, reassuringly unrevealing. But the utterances of Georges's mother appear just as futile and illusive, and the words exchanged by Georges and Blum or by de Reixach and his lieutenant are often said to be hollow (165, 232, 244–45, 274–75).

If it fails in its epistemologico-descriptive function, language also fails in its communicative function. Indeed, because the same words are employed to designate different things, because generic categories are used to refer to particulars, they erect formidable barriers between their users and constitute a major obstacle to communication (see 60, 123, 165, 305). Similarly, written history, which serves victorious nations, pedigreed families, and disinfected textbooks (188, 214–15), seems incapable of capturing the individual, the unique, the real. Based on such bankrupt notions as continuity, order, rationality, and progress—notions belied by the Flanders debacle—history overlooks accidents and suppresses contradictions. It favors simple explanations and tidy patterns, conventional motivations and well-worn scripts (70, 144, 187–88, 307). It adopts the tricks of narrative, sacrificing accuracy for tellability and facts for effects: "unless this simply happened to him while he was cleaning his pistol, which occurs frequently, but in that case there would be no story at least no story sensational enough for your mother to have filled your ears with it and those of her guests" (84). Most generally, books, the visions they impart, the knowledge they purport to preserve, develop, and convey, may prove inane when measured against life. Rousseau's two dozen volumes amount, perhaps, to little more than tearful prose, confused sermons on universal fraternity, gushing and silly developments on the idyllic reign of Reason and Virtue (83, 201, 202, 312). Georges's father, who firmly believes in the incomparable achievements of Western civilization ("he is convinced that there is no problem, and in particular that of the happiness of humanity, which can't be solved by reading good authors," 222), bemoans the destruction of the Leipzig library; but the thousands of writings in that library could not protect their home (223, 224–25). Besides, in many contexts—that of the prison camp, for example—books are less valuable than socks and underwear, cigarettes and soap, chocolate, sugar, and salami (224–25). In fact, the Jewish pimp who quietly dominates his fellow prisoners does not know how to read (220–21), and

Blum shows much more experience than Georges, who has studied too many books and believed too many fictions (131, 169).

Because Simon's text appears to constitute a sort of "disorderly and incoherent choir, of Babelesque gabbling" (56), because the narrative problematizes narrator(s) and narratee(s) (exactly who is speaking to whom?), narration and narrated (gaps, holes, confusions, contradictions, digressions, transgressions); because words in *La Route des Flandres* seem unable to do many things, it could be argued that Simon uses them to undo everything. The subject matter of history would turn out to be the perpetual return of the same fateful chaos; historiography would always emerge as a mere series of pious fictions; and language would primarily function as object rather than as sign and make up antirepresentational texts instead of representational messages. Yet Simon said of his novel that it could have been called "Fragmentary Description of a Disaster," which suggests that representation can be considered one of the ends of the work, though perhaps not the main one.[5] Furthermore, the ability of passage after passage—the horse race, the death of Wack, the lovemaking between Corinne and Georges, the card game in the prison camp—to see or to show seems to me undeniable. Finally, many aspects of *La Route des Flandres* imply and even thematize the possibility of histories and the possibilities of language. The novel multiplies uncertainties without eliminating certainty (or, at least, levels thereof). It privileges repetition without erasing difference and destroying hierarchy. The Napoleonic retreat from Spain, for instance, is not equivalent to the Flanders catastrophe. Whatever the nature and causes of the ancestor's death, the circumstances surrounding it are distinct from those surrounding the death of de Reixach. History is not an undifferentiated magma. Some things happened, incontrovertibly and uniquely. De Reixach's regiment was annihilated. He died. Georges spent time in a prison camp. Whether Iglesia slept with Corinne is more uncertain; whether their possible affair led to the captain's end is even more dubious; and whether that end is non-contingently related to the ancestor's fate is, at best, highly problematic. What *La Route des Flandres* puts into question is not so much the reality or singularity of situations and events as their semiotic autonomy and finality and their acontextual totalization. What it underlines is not the inanity of knowledge but its limits and limitations.

The telling of events by means of a narration that emphasizes sequence in what is or may be simultaneous, that stresses the distinction of moments at the expense of their confusion, that separates what happens from what is perceived, remembered, dreamed, imagined, or hypothesized, amounts to an interested myth. The conception and writing of History with a capital H, of legal history with its reductionism, univocality, claims to transcendence and definitiveness, and subservience to predictable narrative modes, is untenable; it is no less a fable or a farce than is a notion like Providence (187–88). On the other hand (here it should be noted that Georges and Blum do not readily abandon their attempt at understanding, just as it should be noted that Simon's novel stubbornly pursues reformulation and redefinition), maybe a transgressive, self-conscious, and self-critical history is possible. It would aspire to no ordering other than temporary, no synthesis other than provisional, no conclusion other than situated. And without renouncing narrative it would substitute openness for closure; problematize communicational circuits; question beginnings, middles, ends; favor rupture instead of continuity, simultaneity and not succession, metaphoric rather than metonymic relata;

and generally work toward the tearing down of conventional barriers.

To a nonlegal history there must correspond a nonlegal narrative: "that is to say not an idyll, an intrigue unfolding, verbose, conventional, orderly, beginning, growing, developing according to a harmonious and reasonable crescendo interrupted by the indispensable pauses and false moves, and a culminating point, and after that perhaps a plateau, and after that still the obligatory decrescendo: nothing organized, nothing coherent . . . only that . . . all unformulated—and even unformed—and therefore that simple series of gestures, words, insignificant scenes" (50–51). There must be discovered and invented an unofficial language, a polyvocal language for that which usually has no language—singularity, desire, despair—a language that would attempt to say what should be said, accident and difference, conflict, contradiction, and disaster. This is not utopian, according to *La Route des Flandres*. In the first place, the distance between narrative and life, story and experience, words and things is not quite unbridgeable: "so that we would have become without realizing it something like beasts, it seems to me that I have read somewhere a story like that guys metamorphosed with the tap of a wand into pigs or trees or pebbles, the whole thing by means of Latin verses. . . . And so he is not entirely wrong. And so in short words are good for something after all, so that in his cottage he can probably persuade himself that by dint of combining them in every possible way one can after all manage sometimes with a little luck to get it right" (100). Whence Simon's reluctance to "disnarrate" and his affinity for multiple versions and reformulations. In the second place, the novel makes it clear that language, for all its insufficiencies, should not be too quickly dismissed. Reveling in its failures proves no wiser than extolling its perfections. The valorization of the nonlinguistic or antilinguistic is criticized. When Georges, evoking the destruction of the Leipzig library, argues that books are useless, Blum interrupts him: "O.K. Right. O.K. Right. We know" (225). And the protagonist himself comes to realize that his quest for certainty and understanding beyond language is as foolish as his father's unconditional allegiance to words: "it would not be this way that is with her or rather through her that I would reach it . . . perhaps it was as futile, as empty of sense of reality as to align scrawls on sheets of paper and to look for it in words" (295).[6]

Language (narrative language) can, in fact, be useful. By allowing for the construction of an indefinite number of possible worlds, it can help to illuminate one or more aspects of our ever changing reality and even to prepare us for new states of affairs in that reality: "I will tell him that I had already read in Latin what happened to me, which means that I was not too surprised and even to a certain extent reassured to know that it had already been written down, so that all the money he too spent to make me learn it won't have been completely wasted either" (100). But language, through its magic, can also help us to escape intolerable situations or to make them more palatable: "words invented in the hope of making edible—like those vaguely sugared pastes with which one conceals bitter medicines from children—the unnamable reality . . . sounds, noise to ward off the cold, the rails, the livid sky, the somber pines" (184). If it often seems communicatively inadequate, this is perhaps not so much because of some essential incapacity but, rather, because communication circuits are far more complicated than we would like to believe: "Then he stopped. It was not his father he wanted to talk to. It was not even the woman lying invisible by his side, perhaps it was not even Blum to whom he was explaining, whispering in the dark, that if the sun had not hidden they would have known which side their shadows were on" (100).

As for referential adequacy, it too may be a function of not taking the appropriateness and transparency of linguistic forms for granted. There is a *mieux dire* in *La Route des Flandres* ("Georges and Blum reconstituted gradually, bit by bit or more accurately onomatopoeia by onomatopoeia . . . the entire story," 67); there are better ways of expressing certain things, and the text looks for them untiringly (*comment dire, comment appeler ça, comment appellent-ils ça*) and sometimes suggests that it may have found them (*à vrai dire, c'est le cas de le dire, je dis bien*).[7] Its very nature puts language on the side of convention. The real, on the contrary, is a tangled profusion of singularities. The relation between words and things can simply not be simple; and, to approach particulars linguistically, one must beware of scripts, go beyond readily available phrases and well-worn expressions ("in the village square, that is, the rectangle of black mud around the drinking trough," 123), dare to be improper ("I could hear it . . . saying: . . . nasty business . . . I had forgotten that this kind of thing was simply called a 'business' . . . a delicate euphemism a more discreet more elegant formula well so much the better nothing was lost yet since we were still among well-bred people say do not say, example do not say 'the squadron got massacred in an ambush,' but 'we had some lively business outside the village of,' " 165), and realize that utterances should be completed by an indefinite number of "et ceteras." Simon multiplies the "et ceteras" and fills them out. Not for him discretion and understatement (words are usually litotes for things); not for him the smooth locution, the finished statement, the i without a dot, the t without a bar. Perhaps a look at his use of *c'est-à-dire* ("that is," "that is to say") will allow me further to specify his manner and what it signals.

I counted 177 occurrences of *c'est-à-dire* in *La Route des Flandres*, which, according to my calculations, comes to well over one per every two pages. Of course, this may not seem remarkable, given the linguistic fabric of Simon's novel. Many readers and critics have noted that the interpretation of situations and events occupies more space than their representation; many have drawn attention to the improvisational look and metalinguistic character of the novelist's discourse; many have commented on the proliferation of repair terms, the multiplicity of hesitations, adjustments, corrections, and reformulations, the abundance of such terms as *sans doute, comme si, peut-être, ou, ou plutôt, ou au moins, ou en tout cas, pour ainsi dire*, and *si l'on peut dire*.[8] Bernard Pingaud, for example, asserted early on that the language of *La Route des Flandres* mainly foregrounded itself; Dominique Lancereaux showed how Simonian writing constituted a quest for its own being; in a justly famous article Jean Ricardou argued that the novel's linguistic order replaced the order of logic and chronology and the disorder of numerous routs. Claude Simon himself insisted that "one never writes—or says—anything other than what takes place *in the present* of writing"; he praised the self-generating power of words, and maintained that what a text ultimately narrates is how it becomes a text.[9] The number of *c'est-à-dire*'s, then, may not be exceptionally high in the context of the work.[10] But this makes it easier to study the functioning of the locution.

Besides, as much as or even more than the other repair terms Claude Simon shows fondness for, *c'est-à-dire* emphasizes the importance of interpretation in *La Route des Flandres*. It is, after all, the interpretive expression par excellence.[11] As much as the other repair terms, too, *c'est-à-dire* signifies that metalanguage is an integral part of language (which always leads me to more language!); it constitutes a (potential) starting point for the digressions that make up most of Simon's text (interjecting parentheticals—e.g., 12, 18, 26—it is often doubled by a parenthesis or a dash); it underscores the difficulty of expressing, of finding the right word, of designating the right thing (the specifications and definitions introduced by *c'est-à-dire* are themselves frequently specified and explained: "though I'm afraid that it did not happen according to rule, that is, in the right way, that is, hit by an enemy aiming at me in the position of the kneeling shooter," 99; "for him yesterday just now and tomorrow have definitively ceased to exist that is to preoccupy him that is to bother him," 105–6). Moreover, it institutes a scene of reading: not only is it prelude to the reformulation of something preceding it; it also urges readers to identify this something. The *c'*—the "that"—proves particularly opaque: "about half the squadron finding itself caught when they flowed back toward the crossroads, that is, like an accordion" (155); "and between his palm and the silky skin of the arm, still something, no thicker than a leaf of cigarette paper, but something intervening, that is, the sensation of touching experienced as slightly delayed, as when the fingers numbed by the cold rest on an object and perceive it only, it seems, through a film, a kind of shell of insensibility" (238).

Indeed, *c'est-à-dire* is not only characteristic of the general manner of *La Route des Flandres* but also emblematic of its particular matter. The novel (which — like *A, c'est-à-dire B* — consists of three parts) falls under the sign of rectification (as evidenced by the opening epigraph: "I thought I was learning how to live, I was learning how to die"), and Simon has pointed out that the first fifteen or twenty pages provide a kind of global view of "the Flanders road," whereas the nearly three hundred pages that follow represent a deepening of that view.[12] More specifically, the novel can be said to comprise a series of retellings—by Georges, by Blum, by an elusive narrative voice—of events that bear a strong family resemblance but are fundamentally dissimilar (the rout in Spain and that in Flanders, the death of the ancestor and that of de Reixach, the sexual transgression of the peasant woman and that of Corinne); it can be said to be made up of a series of repetitions with a difference, miniaturized and reflected in the form *A, c'est-à-dire B*. It makes use of both first- and third-person narration and of neither (Merleau-Ponty spoke of an intermediate voice),[13] once again paralleled by *c'est-à-dire*, which falls between *je veux dire* and *cela veut dire* ("I mean to say" and "it means"), between the speaker as responsible source and the reformulation of semantic but not pragmatic or enunciative content. It proceeds along a set of divisions and fractures (past and present, conjecture and fact, prison camp and hotel room, horse race and cavalry squadron, not to mention the Flanders road, which of course is a *via rupta*, a broken way), and *c'est-à-dire* institutes a ruptured discourse. Finally, many of its themes find a sort of linguistic correlative in the form I am considering. There is the theme of immutability and change, for example: *c'est-à-dire* does not annul what precedes it but takes one beyond. There is the theme of longing for total vision: if *c'est-à-dire* divides, it also bridges the left and the right, what comes before and what comes after; Georges, evoking de Reixach's death, speaks of the "patient murderer finger on the trigger seeing so to speak the back of what I could see or I the back and he the front, that is, between the two of us I following him and the other one watching him advance we possessed the totality of the enigma (the murderer knowing what was going to happen to him and I knowing what had happened to him, that is, after and before, that is, like the two halves of an orange that's been split and that fit together perfectly)" (313). Above all, there is the triple theme of language, narrative, and understanding.

Contrary to the many other repair terms in *La Route des Flandres* (Simon uses more than fifty), *c'est-à-dire* not only announces a reformulation but also connotes the duty to reformulate. The locution can be read as meaning simply "that is to say," "that is," "that signifies"; but it can be said as well to involve a deontic modality as in *c'est à faire, c'est à régler* ("that is to be done," "that is to be settled"): *c'est-à-dire* or "that is to be said," "one must say," "it is necessary to say," if the thing is to be expressed, if the state of affairs is to be grasped, if understanding is to occur. This sense of obligation finds itself reaffirmed throughout the novel. Though the distribution of *c'est-à-dire* varies, the changes are not particularly significant. It is true that the central and longest part exhibits the highest proportion of the term (one *c'est-à-dire* per 1.4 pages, as opposed to one per 2 pages in the first part and one per 2.2 pages in the final section, where it becomes increasingly clear that Georges's quest will fail and where the protagonist increasingly realizes it); but it is also true that we find a very high proportion in the last fifteen pages (thirteen, or almost one to a page). Nor is the sense of obligation linked to a particular voice in the novel: *c'est-à-dire* appears in first- and third-person narration as well as in the dialogues between Iglesia, Georges, and Blum. Once again, the differences are not decisive. There are proportionally more tokens in third-person narration (seemingly the most impersonal of voices): one per 1.5 pages as compared to one per 2.3 pages in the first-person narration and one per 1.6 pages in dialogues. But it is a participant in the last, Blum, who shows the greatest fondness for the locution: one per 1.4 pages.[14]

If *c'est-à-dire* connotes the necessity to express in certain ways, it also establishes—along with many other repair terms, this time—a hierarchy resting on a presupposed common norm. The terms linked by the locution may be and most often are ontically equivalent, designating the same object, but they prove communicatively different. In *A, c'est-à-dire B,* A and B are not reversible. The second term is the better one, more adequate than the first, less semiotically problematic, closer to accurate formulation and successful communication. *C'est-à-dire* can, of course, fulfill a number of distinct functions. It can introduce a restriction or a refusal, for example, as in "Vous pouvez y aller, c'est-à-dire si vous le désirez" or "—Tu viens?— C'est-à-dire que je suis très occupé." It can institute or underline an ironic effect, as in "Il y faisait très froid, c'est-à-dire que la température n'y dépassait jamais les 40 degrés Celsius." It can order a series of (oral-like) discourse sequences or at least simulate a kind of order. But its main function is to allow for the redefinition or reformulation of a term that is overly technical ("un voilier encalminé, c'est-à-dire arrêté par le manque de vent"), referentially inadequate ("il y a trois semaines, c'est-à-dire il y a un mois"), or, most generally, insufficiently informative.[15]

Now in *La Route des Flandres, c'est-à-dire* functions classically. Not only is it rarely, if ever, redundant (suggesting that language yields mere prattle, disconcerting receivers instead of helping them); it is never employed to mark negation or refusal, seldom—four or five times and mainly in relation to Blum—used as a sign of linguistic verve or superficial order (see 184–85, 194, 312), and in only about a dozen instances mobilized for ironic or comic effect: "he knew that Blum had chanced upon the better share (that is, the one that must have weighed about five or six grams more than the other) (76); "a woman (that is, all the same, a human being)" (182); "the artist's know-how, that is, his knowing good manners, that is, his knowing how to flatter" (196). In 85 percent of the cases, *c'est-à-dire* introduces definitional reformulations, interpretive refinements, specifications, and explanations that are sometimes rather lengthy (137, 184, 300) and often pertain to the more salient concerns and the more striking motifs of the novel: the dead horse, the quest, woman, time, death, history, disaster. These reformulations and refinements do not usually constitute a response to the technical nature of a given expression; I found only two possible examples: "bay-brown that is to say almost black" (301) and "one of the five animals forging . . . that is hitting the toe of its left hind foot against the heel of its right front foot at trotting pace" (302). Nor do they habitually result from the idiosyncratic or private use of a particular word or phrase; again, I found only two possible examples (12, 26). Unlike Céline, whose works also contain many reformulations, Simon does not generally proceed from the more spontaneous and personal to the more artificial and public. Most interestingly, perhaps, the repairs following *c'est-à-dire* are not, by and large, the consequence of referentially inadequate terms—no more than eight times (e.g., 82, 142, 255). Referring does not constitute a problem in *La Route des Flandres*, and *c'est-à-dire* serves extensional as well as intensional purposes and introduces additional information on things at least as often as on words. The difficulty is that what is named is not so much a "thing" as a "named thing." Referents have always already been referred to. This is the condition underlined by the profusion of *c'est-à-dire*'s (and other repair terms) as well as by the abundance of retellings: I cannot get *out* of language (*out* of narrative) and get *to* the thing (*to* the event), and in order to capture some of the specificity of the latter, I must multiply designations (stories) for what is already a designation (a story).

Simon's two-phased or, rather, multiphased writing—no fewer than twenty-six repairs introduced by *c'est-à-dire* are themselves reformulated through a new *c'est-à-dire*—simultaneously signals the problem of redoing things with words and the determination to try by redoing words with words. It indefatigably goes from the conventional to the contextual, the schematic to the detailed, the unfocused to the adjusted, and illustrates the possibility of exploring and reinventing with words the very things that will always outdo them. It promotes (and constitutes) a narrative without narrativity, one that eschews positiveness (this happened, then that; this happened because of that; this happened, and it was related to that) and totalization ("without beginning or end or landmarks," 30) and that, through repeated approximations and hesitant retellings, becomes an analog to the debacle and dissolution it can never definitively grasp or explain. In other words, if one wanted to learn more about disaster and the particularities of disasters, one could always read *La Route des Flandres*.

10... Narrative All the Same

In Patrick Modiano's *Rue des Boutiques Obscures*, an amnesiac private eye (an amnesiac private "I") who has been given the name "Guy Roland" (along with papers and a passport) by Constantin Hutte, his boss for eight years and now his friend, attempts to recover his identity.[1] He is the missing person who must be located.[2] At the beginning of the novel, some time around 1965, ten years have passed since Guy Roland lost his memory (15). He finds a new track to follow, and this is the partial story he reconstructs (we reconstruct). Born on September 30, 1912, in Salonica, Greece, Jimmy Pedro Stern went to the Collège de Luiza et d'Albany, an exclusive French private school. There, he became friends with Freddie Howard de Luz. In the 1930s he had a legal address in Rome—2, rue des Boutiques Obscures—but lived in Paris where he worked as a broker (180) and where he apparently consorted with the idle rich, fallen Russian aristocrats, café society, the demimonde. In April 1939 he married Denise Coudreuse, a young French model and later a dress designer. He disappeared in 1940 to reappear as Pedro McEvoy (note that the author has the same initials)—a Dominican subject employed by his country's legation in occupied Paris—and live the dangerous life of the foreigner with fake credentials. By the end of 1942, Pedro and Denise, along with Freddie, his wife Gay Orlow, and an ex-jockey friend by the name of André Wildmer, leave Paris for Megève, near the Swiss border: Denise is the only one whose papers are in order (she is the only French citizen among them), and they will all be safer there. But in Megève, Pedro continues to experience dread. He decides to cross the border clandestinely with Denise. Bob Besson, a ski instructor, and Oleg de Wrédé, a young man of Russian origin and dubious occupation, promise to help them for 100,000 francs. They leave on February 15, 1943 (120, 178), he with Besson and she with de Wrédé. They are betrayed. Denise vanishes. Pedro resurfaces as Guy Roland.

Of course, things are not that simple (they probably never are). In the first place, "Jimmy Pedro Stern" may well be an assumed name, since the Salonica City Hall archives were destroyed in a fire during World War I and no record from 1912 remains (99). In the second place, there is at least a possibility that Stern and McEvoy are not one and the same person. The two men do have the name Pedro in common; Freddie worked for Stern from 1934 to 1939 (236) and was McEvoy's close friend; Denise married Stern and was McEvoy's companion; Stern disappeared and McEvoy appeared. But as the text points out, sometimes there are mysterious coincidences (26, 189). Similarly, it is by no means sure that the detective is (was) the former attaché. True, Hélène Pilgram identifies Guy Roland as Pedro McEvoy, though not immediately (108); Wildmer recognizes him (187); and at least two persons have memories that correspond to the protagonist's own (151–52, and 183–85; 170–73, and 208–10). But unlike Pedro, Guy does not smoke, and he wears a moustache. Moreover, four different people do not find that he bears any particular resemblance to the Dominican (45, 69, 79, 91), and he himself does not know what to think. Toward the end of the novel, he writes to Hutte: "I am going to leave Paris next week for an island in the Pacific where I have a chance to meet again a man who will give me information on what my life has been. He may be a friend from my youth. Up to now, everything has seemed so chaotic, so fragmented to me. . . . Bits, scraps of something would come back to me suddenly in the course of my inquiries. . . . But after all, maybe that's what a life is. Is it really mine? or that of another person into which I slipped?" (238). And on the very last page he decides to take one more step and visit an address in Rome: 2, rue des Boutiques Obscures.

Other elements further complicate the protagonist's quest. Thus, Guy Roland meets Stioppa de Djagoriew on a November 5 (27, 30, 39) and learns about Gay Orlow from him. He decides to look for her, and toward the end of October 1965 (53–54) he finds out that she had married and divorced Waldo Blunt, an American musician, and committed suicide in 1950. Almost a year (or two? or three?) must have gone by since Roland saw de Djagoriew. Yet nothing else in the text points to that conclusion. Time is strange, labyrinthian, imprecise. It is a *drôle de temps*, a funny time appropriate to the *drôle d'époque* (114, 172, 210), the funny period that the protagonist is trying to remember or reconstruct, and to the *drôles de gens* (72), the funny people that he meets and may have known. This temporal strangeness and imprecision is intensified by the vagueness of many of the temporal clues provided, the undatable nature of the deictics punctuating the text: "that evening," "it is night time," "yesterday evening" (11, 74, 161). It is also intensified by the seemingly indiscriminate use of both the *passé composé* and the *passé simple* (the tense for a past that is still pertinent to the present and refuses to end, and the tense for a past that is gone), by the adoption of the imperfect when a preterit may be expected (with the former, boundaries vanish and instants dilate), and by the ambiguity of many a present (e.g., 74–75: is the present historical or not?). Besides, the temporal status of the narrating is as indefinite as that of the narrated: there are several homodiegetic narrating instances in the novel (see 161), but it is impossible to determine their number; and four of the forty-seven chapters (chapters 26, 32, 34, and 43) feature a covert heterodiegetic narrator rather than a homodiegetic one.

The intricate maze of time is complicated by the bewildering spatial network through which the protagonist moves: "I had discovered in this maze of staircases and elevators, among these hundreds of cells, a man who perhaps . . ." (46); "In this maze of streets and boulevards, we had met one day, Denise Coudreuse and I" (147). It is a network enveloped and eroded by fog (49, 50, 132, 219), steam, snow ("The echo of our gestures and of our lives, it seemed to me that it was smothered by this cotton wool which fell around us," 225), and it is further complicated by the labyrinth of memory: "The events preceding our departure for Megève come back to me, in bits and scraps. The big illuminated windows of the former Hôtel Zaharoff, on Avenue Hoche, the disconnected sentences of Wildmer, and the names . . . and the other impalpable details . . . all these things are for me like Ariadne's thread" (208).[3] In and through memory, dates, places, objects, persons are mingled and fused (242). A face is preserved but not the name attached to it. A name persists but not the man or woman it designates. An incident remains but not the circumstances surrounding it (122, 124, 165). Nor is it clear how and why people remember what they want to forget and forget what they hope to remember (176), how and why certain images survive and others fade, how and why they evoke some things and not others. Besides, it is not only the items memory selects and the itineraries it follows that are baffling. Its very nature is problematic, since to distinguish recalling from imagining or reconstructing is frequently impossible: "We had left very early, that morning.... It was sunny *since* Denise was wearing a big straw hat" (151).[4] "To see in one's memory" can simply mean "to recreate": "Then we went to Giorgiadzé... I saw us walking around noon, down a tree-lined avenue in Nice" (190); and "to remember" can often mean "to tell a story."[5]

If time, place, and memory are strange, so is the protagonist's situation and, more specifically, so are his detecting activities. With the exception of Hutte, Guy Roland seems to have no friends, no relations, no acquaintances; he seems to have no home; he no longer has a job (at the beginning of *Rue des Boutiques Obscures*, Hutte closes the detective agency to retire in Nice); and he often acts as if he did not wish his quest to end. He may be afraid to find out that he is not Pedro McEvoy (it would not be his first disappointment: for over one-third of the novel he wrongly believes that he is Freddie Howard de Luz). He may also be afraid to discover that he is the former Dominican attaché. This Oedipus (Roland, who is looking for his origins, may have been partly responsible for a crime, since the attempt to cross the Swiss border—against Freddie's, Wildmer's, and Gay Orlow's advice, 228–29—was McEvoy's idea) may not want to solve the riddle he faces and constitutes (19). This Theseus may not want to confront the Minotaur. When he meets Hélène Pilgram, for example, there are several questions about his possible life in Paris with Denise which he could ask and does not (chapter 15); when he sees Wildmer, there are many possible lines of inquiry which he fails to pursue (chapter

33); and on the way to Megève he suddenly turns back without attempting to locate the chalet—"Croix du Sud"—where he may have lived (234–35).

Granted, the Megève road Roland thinks he remembers looks like every other mountain road; many chalets are named "Croix du Sud"; and the one McEvoy knew may no longer exist. Moreover, Wildmer himself is quickly exhausted by his conversation with Roland, cuts it off, and forgets his interlocutor (196–97). As for Pilgram, she falls asleep while waiting for Roland to finish a tour of her apartment, an apartment he had possibly shared with Denise (123). Indeed, if the protagonist seems at times to be a specter and to act like one ("I had already lived my life, and I was no more than a ghost floating in the warm air of a Saturday evening," 63), he is not alone. A Japanese man at the bar of the Paris Hilton resembles an embalmed corpse (57); Waldo Blunt seems to be floating in a state of suspended animation (57); and Hutte finds that Nice is "a city of ghosts and specters" (51). Similarly, though the people Guy Roland comes in contact with do not suffer from amnesia, their memory sometimes proves not much better than his. To forget is part of everyone's lot (42, 184, 214). To remember is difficult: "He had made a violent effort to speak of the past with me, but it was over. Like an exhausted swimmer who raises his head above water for the last time and then slowly lets himself sink" (196). After all, ten or twenty years is an eternity ago (22, 26, 129). What happened then happened in another time, a different time, to other, different people. It happened in a time and to people that are *other* (cf.35, 138, 209).

In a certain sense, even if Guy Roland should find the past life that was "really his" (238), that life would not necessarily be more familiar to him—more his own—than another one.

Even if Guy Roland is Pedro McEvoy, he may not have much more in common with him than he would if he were not the Dominican diplomat. Just as there is little in common between "this very tired old man . . . going away into the night with his threadbare coat and his bulky black briefcase and the tennis player of yore, the handsome and blond Baltic baron Constantin von Hutte" (16), there is little in common between who Roland is and who he was, who we are and who we were.

Time passes; things change; we vanish. Everywhere—even in America (49)—people die. Gay Orlow is dead, and Bob Besson, and Rubirosa, and Freddie, perhaps. Everywhere, cultures have been destroyed, tribes scattered, groups dissipated, people exiled; and the characters' migrations (from Mauritius, Russia, or Greece to France, from France to Polynesia or America),[6] as well as the songs they know (*Que reste-t-il de nos amours, Sur les quais du vieux Paris, El Reloj*)[7] and the names they bear (Sonachitzé, Djagoriew, Scouffi, Mansoure, McEvoy), are emblematic of temporal corrosion and spatial dislocation. Little remains of what was. The Howard de Luz castle has been sequestered and devastated. The archives of the Collège de Luiza et d'Albany, like those in Salonica, have been destroyed. The well-named "garage de la Comète" has been closed for years. Little remains of what we were. We are no more, perhaps, than the intersection of vibrations from the past, the crystallization of dispersed echoes floating in the air (124). We have no greater consistency than the fog or the steam on some windowpane (72, 218). We evaporate as quickly as a child's tears (251). We are like the "man on the beach": "In the corners and the background of thousands of vacation pictures, he is figured in a bathing suit in the middle of cheerful groups, but no one could say his name and why he is there. And no one noticed that one day he had disappeared from the pictures. . . . Hutte used to repeat that, at bottom, we are all 'men on the beach' and that 'the sand . . . bears the mark of our steps for only a few seconds' " (72–73).

Some names in old directories or telephone books (which constitute "the most precious and moving library one could have, for they alone bear witness to many of the vanished beings, things, and worlds listed on their pages," 12), a few yellowed photographs, newspaper cuttings, and postcards in a box ("Everything did indeed end up in old chocolate or cookie boxes. Or cigar boxes," 95), two or three worn-out books (Denise Coudreuse devoured classical detective stories, and ironically, Pedro McEvoy often read them too—117, 212—as well as historical memoirs),[8] a strong emotion (such as fear, 98), an address on official documents, an old movie house—these make up what is left of a past, of a life. And a few memories also, uncertain, mysterious, tricky, our own and others' too ("Perhaps something of my life survived, over there, in a little apartment along the gardens, a person who had known me and still remembered me," 241). Of the four chapters exhibiting a heterodiegetic narration, three (chapters 26, 32, 43) adopt the point of view of a minor character (near a beach, in Valparaiso, looking out the window in Paris) whose fleeting memories correspond to or are consistent with Guy Roland's own memories or reconstructions of his past; and one—told in the historical present and from an unsituated point of view—describes the actions of Porfirio Rubirosa, Denise Coudreuse, and Pedro McEvoy in Vichy, probably in 1940 (chapter 34).

Through such bits and scraps, odds and ends, the past—like a ghost—refuses to be left alone. Something happened. The past must not be left alone. Hutte, who argued that it was best to think of the future instead of "looking back" (16), learns that he was wrong and Guy Roland was right: "In life, it is not the future that counts, it is the past" (175). Something happened, and it happened to me: I was, I am. That is the story, Guy Roland's and everyone's story. The past cannot and must not be left alone. It is an imperious need and a frightening duty. With a few shreds and fragments the protagonist hesitantly attempts (one more time) to reconstitute his past, and if memory—his own and that of others—is unreliable, if it fails, there is imagination. There is narrative.

Narrative provides a key to locked doors, supplies material to fill up holes, confers a body to what is even less dense than "the reflection of the moon on an object" (65), creates a web linking and preserving the traces of existents and events. It constitutes a meeting place for scattered voices, "voices from beyond the grave, voices of missing persons, wandering voices" (146–47). It proposes answers to basic questions (who was I? who am I? what happened?). It endows proper names with attributes, thereby giving them a meaning, a life.

Naturally, the key may not be quite suitable. The answer may prove inappropriate or incorrect. Many different narratives can be affixed to the same name (Guy Roland), and many different names can unfold in terms of the same narrative, a possibility underlined by the abundance of hesitant or hypothetical narratives in *Rue des Boutiques Obscures*: "My grandfather Howard de Luz would come get me at the Paris train, or was it the other way around? On summer evenings, I would go wait for him on the station platform together with my grandmother, née Mabel Donahue" (82). After all, there are (there were) countless people who could at any moment be asked for their papers, rounded up, tortured, deported, killed; countless people who owned a number of passports and acquired a number of identities ("in life, one must take precautions and always have several passports," 111); countless people for whom accident took on the look of fate, who were younger then and are older now and have lost their own traces. Even when I find a narrative that fits me, it may be falsified: "There! it was clear! my name was not Freddie Howard de Luz. ... I had never taken a walk along this lawn with an American grandmother. I had never, as a child, played in the 'labyrinth.' This rusted beam, with its swings, had not been erected for me. Too bad" (92). And it can never be definitively confirmed, since new details can always come to light and bring new light ("I had to try one last step: visit my old address in Rome, 2, rue des Boutiques Obscures," 251) and since new connections can always be established: for instance, between the restaurant that Guy Roland goes to early in the novel and the bungalow that he remembers some time later (19, 151).

Guy Roland has read many detective stories; he has also read many books of memoirs; and he even knows L. de Viel Castel's history of the French Revolution in seventeen volumes (151). But his own narrative and *Rue des Boutiques Obscures* do not resemble them. Not for him the itinerary from baffling enigma to reassuring solution, the successful integration of past and present, the ingenious reconstruction of an entire era. Though the novel includes several stock elements of detective fiction, for example (a bout with amnesia, good leads that turn out to be bad ones, crucial but unlocatable witnesses, and so on),[9] it subverts their usual function(ing) by finally refusing to solve the protagonist's problem. It opts instead for fragmentariness. It rejects totalization. It resists closure. Though barely 240 (short) pages long, the novel is divided into forty-seven chapters, some of which (chapters 19, 41) consist of a couple of lines and many of which comprise a large number of sections: chapter 37, the longest, runs to twenty-four pages but is made up of twenty different parts. At the macrotextual level, the whiteness invading many of the pages—the multiplicity of blanks occasioned by the numerous chapters and sections—thus repeats, as it were, and emphasizes the whiteness of the snow that (may have) engulfed Pedro and Denise ("I ended up lying down in the snow. All around me, there was no longer anything but whiteness," 231) and the blankness of amnesia. At the microtextual level, moreover, preference is frequently given to simple sentential juxtaposition over subordination or even coordination. Furthermore, the multiple points of view orienting the presentation of events as well as the shifts from first-person to third-person narration and the heterogeneity of the texts constituting Guy Roland's story (postcards, letters, pages from a directory, telephone numbers, official documents, and so on) frustrate any ultimate summing up. Finally, the last pages of the novel underline its open-endedness.[10]

The past is not recaptured. The self is not illuminated. The riddle cannot be solved. Though it does provide a fragile sketch of or blueprint for the (re)construction of a life or a world, narrative does not fully restore what was and does not conquer time, forgetfulness, and death. But perhaps, from a narrative point of view, these failures are not to be deplored. After all and paradoxically, they can be said to signify narrative's mimetic power and adequacy, since they reflect the elusiveness, discontinuity, and problematic nature of life and self. Besides, the primary function and importance of narrative may well be semiotic rather than mimetic, or even constitutive rather than imitative. If narrative is the (imperfect) record of something that happened, even more it is the manifestation, recognition, and reminder that something happened. If narrative represents (my) life, even more it constitutes it.

Notes

ONE: ON THEME AND THEMING

1. Norman Friedman, *Form and Meaning in Fiction* (Athens: University of Georgia Press, 1975), p.56.
2. The colloquium "Pour une thématique" was sponsored by the Ecole des Hautes Etudes en Sciences Sociales, supported by the Centre National de la Recherche Scientifique and held in June 1984 at the Centre Culturel Canadien in Paris. See Viviane Alleton, Claude Bremond, and Thomas Pavel, "Vers une thématique," *Poétique*, no.64 (1985): 396.
3. On theme, see, among many others, Monroe Beardsley, *Aesthetics: Problems in the Philosophy of Criticism* (New York: Harcourt, Brace, 1958); Claude Bremond, "Concept et thème," *Poétique*, no.64 (1985): 415–23; Menachem Brinker, "Thème et interprétation," *Poétique*, no.64 (1985): 435–43; Seymour Chatman, "On the Notion of Theme in Narrative," in John Fisher, ed., *Essays in Aesthetics: Perspectives on the Work of Monroe C. Beardsley* (Philadelphia: Temple University Press, 1983), pp.161–79; Horst S. Daemmrich and Ingrid Daemmrich, *Themes and Motifs in Western Literature: A Handbook* (Tübingen: Francke, 1986); František Daneš, "Functional Sentence Perspective and the Organization of the Text," in František Daneš, ed., *Papers on Functional Sentence Perspective* (Prague: Academic Publishing House of the Czechoslovak Academy of Sciences, 1974), pp.106–28; Teun A. van Dijk, *Text and Context* (London: Longman, 1977); Oswald Ducrot and Tzvetan Todorov, *Dictionnaire encyclopédique des sciences du*

langage (Paris: Seuil, 1972); Eugene H. Falk, *Types of Thematic Structure* (Chicago: University of Chicago Press, 1967); Michael D. Fortescue, *A Discourse Production Model . . . for "Twenty Questions"* (Amsterdam: John Benjamins, 1980); Elizabeth Frenzel, *Stoff-, Motif-, und Symbolforschung*, 4th ed. (Stuttgart: Metzler, 1978); Philippe Hamon, "Thème et effet de réel," *Poétique*, no.64 (1985): 495–503; Larry Bert Jones, *Pragmatic Aspects of English Text Structure* (Dallas, Tex.: SIL Publications in Linguistics, (1983); Linda Kay Jones, *Theme in English Expository Discourse* (Lake Bluff, Ill.: Jupiter Press, 1977); Charles N. Li, ed., *Subject and Topic* (New York: Academic Press, 1976); Jean-Pierre Richard, *Microlectures* (Paris: Seuil, 1979); Shlomith Rimmon-Kenan, "Qu'est-ce qu'un thème?" *Poétique*, no.64 (1985): 397–406; Raymond Trousson, *Le Thème de Prométhée dans la littérature européenne*, 2 vols. (Geneva: Droz, 1964); Alexander Zholkovsky, *Themes and Texts: Toward a Poetics of Expressiveness* (Ithaca, N.Y.: Cornell University Press, 1984). It will become clear, I hope, that my discussion of theme and theming also owes a lot to Roland Barthes, *S/Z* (Paris: Seuil, 1970).

4. Dijk uses "topic" and "theme" interchangeably; see *Text and Context*, pp.130–35.

5. In more "ordinary" English, it might be rendered: "A proposition T is a topic of a sequence of propositions Σ equivalent to $<p_1, p_2, \ldots p_n>$ if and only if for each p_i that is part of Σ there is a subsequence Σ_k of Σ such that p_i is part of Σ_k and for each successive Σ_k there is a p_j such that Σ_k entails p_j and T entails p_j."

6. See Dijk, *Text and Context*, p.136.

7. See Nelson Goodman, "About," in his *Problems and Projects* (Indianapolis, Ind.: Bobbs-Merrill, 1972), 246–72; and Hilary Putnam, "Formalization of the Concept 'About,'" *Philosophy of Science* 25 (1958): 125–30.

8. See P. F. Strawson, "Identifying References and Truth Values,"

Theoria 30 (1964): 96–118; and Tanya Reinhart, *Pragmatics and Linguistics: An Analysis of Sentence Topics* (Bloomington: Indiana University Linguistic Club, 1982).

9. On the notion of "relevance," see Dan Sperber and Deirdre Wilson, *Relevance: Communication and Cognition* (Oxford: Basil Blackwell, 1986).

10. I take these two terms to be interchangeable.

11. Honoré de Balzac, *Eugénie Grandet* (Paris: Garnier, 1965). All page references in the text are to this edition.

12. According to Deirdre Wilson and Dan Sperber, "On Grice's Theory of Conversation," in Paul Werth, ed., *Conversation and Discourse: Structure and Interpretation* (New York: St. Martin's Press, 1981), pp.167, 177, proposition Q constitutes a pragmatic implication of proposition P if, together with a context C, P logically implies Q, but P by itself does not logically imply Q, and C by itself does not logically imply Q. Wilson and Sperber also note that the "logic used in deriving pragmatic implications must in fact be more restricted than standard logics in at least one respect: it must lack certain 'trivial' inference rules contained in most standard logics. The 'trivial' rules are those that (a) apply to any proposition at all, regardless of its form and content, and hence (b) may reapply an indefinite number of times given a single initial premise or pair of premises. With the exclusion of these rules, the pragmatic implications of a given proposition will always be finite, given a finite set of premises." Given two propositions P and Q, "trivial" inference rules leading to such implications as P & Q, P v Q, P & P & Q & Q, etc., would therefore not apply.

13. Naomi Schor, "Pour une thématique restreinte: Ecriture, parole, et différence dans *Madame Bovary*," *Littérature*, no.22 (1976): 30–46.

TWO: THE THEME OF NARRATIVE

1. Michel Charles, *L'Arbre et la source* (Paris: Seuil, 1985), p.35.

2. See Antti Aarne, *The Types of the Folktale: A Classification and Bibli-*

ography, trans. and enlarged Stith Thompson (Helsinki: Suomolainen Tiedeakatemia, 1961); and Aarne, *Motif-Index of Folk-Literature*, rev. and enlarged Stith Thompson (Bloomington: Indiana University Press, 1955–58).

3. Gerald Prince, "*Le Nœud de vipères*, ou Les destinations d'un récit," *Orbis Litterarum* 21 (1976): 72–78; and Prince, "Récit et texte dans *Le Moyen de parvenir*," *Neophilologus* 65 (1981): 1–5.

4. Jean Ricardou, "L'Histoire dans l'histoire," in *Problèmes du nouveau roman* (Paris: Seuil, 1967), p.178; Tzvetan Todorov, "La Quête du récit: *Le Graal*," in *Poétique de la prose (choix): Suivi de Nouvelles recherches sur le récit* (Paris: Seuil, 1978), p.79; Barthes, *S/Z*, pp.96, 219.

5. Marthe Robert, *Roman des origines et origines du roman* (Paris: Grasset, 1972), p.67.

6. Apart from the Russian Formalists and Marthe Robert, Barthes, Ricardou, and Todorov, I have drawn on Peter Brooks, *Reading for the Plot: Design and Intention in Narrative* (New York: Knopf, 1984); Ross Chambers, *Meaning and Meaningfulness* (Lexington, Ky.: French Forum, 1979), and Chambers, *Story and Situation: Narrative Seduction and the Power of Fiction* (Minneapolis: University of Minnesota Press, 1984); Lucien Dällenbach, *Le Récit spéculaire* (Paris: Seuil, 1977); Jean-Pierre Faye, *Le Récit hunique* (Paris: Seuil, 1967); Linda Hutcheon, *Narcissistic Narrative: The Metafictional Paradox* (New York: Methuen, 1984); Roman Jakobson, "Closing Statement: Linguistics and Poetics," in Thomas A. Sebeok, ed., *Style in Language* (New York: Wiley, 1960), pp.350–77; and Jean Verrier, "Le Récit réfléchi," *Littérature*, no.5 (1972): 58–68.

7. See Barthes, *S/Z*; Todorov, "Le Récit primitif: *L'Odyssée*," "Les Hommes-récits: *Les Mille et une nuits*," and "La Quête du récit: *Le Graal*," in *Poétique de la prose*, pp.21–32, 33–46, 59–80; and Brooks, *Reading for the Plot*, pp.84–87.

8. See Thomas Pavel, "Le Déploiement de l'intrigue," *Poétique*, no.64

(1985): 455–61. See also Jean Rousset, *Forme et signification: Essais sur les structures littéraires de Corneille à Claudel* (Paris: Corti, 1962).

9. Hamon, "Thème et effet de réel," p.405.

10. See Zholkovsky, *Themes and Texts*.

11. Marc Angenot, "Rupture et narration: Sur le 'récit dans le récit,'" *Degrés*, no.2 (1973): n4.

12. These other operations are augmentation, variation, contrast, coordination, combination, preparation, and reduction.

13. See Barthes, *S/Z*, p.100.

THREE: THE DISNARRATED

1. See Jonathan Culler, *Structuralist Poetics: Structuralism, Linguistics, and the Study of Literature* (Ithaca, N.Y.: Cornell University Press, 1975), p.143.

2. I have also thought of calling this third category *alternarrated*. But, all things considered, I believe that *disnarrated* is the more appropriate term.

3. See Victor Shklovsky, "Art and Technique," in Lee T. Lemon and Marion J. Reis, eds., *Russian Formalist Criticism* (Lincoln: University of Nebraska Press, 1965), pp.3–24; Claude Bremond, *Logique du récit* (Paris: Seuil, 1973), p.22; William Labov, *Language in the Inner City* (Philadelphia: University of Pennsylvania Press, 1972), chap.9; Mary Louise Pratt, *Toward a Speech Act Theory of Literary Discourse* (Bloomington: Indiana University Press, 1977), esp. pp.49–50, 65–68, 72–73; and Marie-Laure Ryan, "Embedded Narratives and Tellability," *Style* 20 (1986): 319–40.

4. Cf. Jean Sareil, "La Description négative," *Romanic Review* 78 (1987): 1–9.

5. See Bremond, *Logique du récit*.

6. See Ryan, "Embedded Narratives"; and Labov, *Language in the Inner City*, chap.9 .

7. On this subject, see Gerald Prince, "Remarques sur le *topos* et sur le dénarré," in Nicole Boursier and David Trott, eds., *La Naissance du roman en France* (Paris: Biblio 17, 1990), pp.113–22.

FOUR: SINGULAR NARRATIVE

1. Madame de La Fayette, *La Princesse de Clèves* (Paris: Librairie Générale de France, 1958). All page references are to this edition.
2. For a "grammatical" account of such linkage operations, see Gerald Prince, *Narratology: The Form and Functioning of Narrative* (Berlin: Walter de Gruyter, 1982), pp.88–92.
3. One possible story that the novel's characters do not envision is a story in which the heroine's love for M. de Nemours fades and dies.
4. My discussion is particularly indebted to Mireille Calle-Gruber, "*La Princesse de Clèves*, ou: Du refus d'être (la) fable de récits," *Degrés*, no.41 (1985): d1–d26; Joan DeJean, "Lafayette's Ellipses: The Privileges of Anonymity," PMLA 99 (1984): 884–902; Juliette Frølich, "*La Princesse de Clèves* ou la magie du conte," *Orbis Litterarum* 34 (1979): 208–26; Gérard Genette, "Vraisemblance et motivation," *Communications*, no.11 (1968): 5–21; Laurence A. Gregorio, *Order in the Court: History and Society in "La Princesse de Clèves"* (Saratoga, Calif.: Anma Libri, 1986); Dalia Judovitz, "The Aesthetics of Implausibility: *La Princesse de Clèves*," MLN, 99 (1984): 1037–56; Donna Kuizenga, *Narrative Strategies in "La Princesse de Clèves"* (Lexington, Ky.: French Forum, 1976); Sylvère Lotringer, "La Structuration romanesque," *Critique*, no.277 (1970): 498–529; John D. Lyons, "Narrative, Interpretation, and Paradox: *La Princesse de Clèves*," *Romanic Review* 72 (1981): 383–400; Nancy K. Miller, "Emphasis Added: Plots and Plausibilities in Women's Fiction," PMLA, 96 (1981): 36–48; Armine Kotin Mortimer, "Narrative Closure and the Paradigm of Self-Knowledge in *La Princesse de Clèves*," *Style* 17 (Spring 1983): 181–95; Richard H. Moye, "Silent Victory: Narrative, Ap-

propriation, and Autonomy in *La Princesse de Clèves*," MLN, 104 (1989), 845–60; Alain Niderst, *"La Princesse de Clèves": Le Roman paradoxal* (Paris: Larousse, 1973); Inge Crosman Wimmers, *Poetics of Reading: Approaches to the Novel* (Princeton, N.J.: Princeton University Press, 1988), pp.24–56.

5. See Maurice Laugaa, *Lectures de Mme de Lafayette* (Paris: Colin, 1971). See also DeJean, "Lafayette's Ellipses"; Genette, "Vraisemblance et motivation"; Judovitz, "The Aesthetics of Implausibility"; Lyons, "Narrative, Interpretation, and Paradox"; and Miller, "Emphasis Added."

6. The paradox of inimitable exemplarity underlines, of course, the heroine's singularity.

7. See Judovitz, "The Aesthetics of Implausibility."

8. See Lyons, "Narrative, Interpretation, and Paradox."

FIVE: CANDID EXPLANATIONS

1. Voltaire, *Candide, ou l'Optimisme*, in *Romans et Contes* (Paris: Garnier, 1960). All page references are to this edition.

2. Jean Sareil, *Essai sur Candide* (Geneva: Droz, 1967), p.83.

3. I am including only those cases in which both the item explained and the explanation are formulated by the same voice. I am also disregarding those passages that may *implicitly* and *indirectly* function as explanations and answer such questions as "What is x?" or "Why is x?" For a quantitative study of *Candide*, see Pierre R. Ducretet and Marie-Paule Ducretet, *Voltaire, Candide: Etude quantitative* (Toronto: University of Toronto Press, 1974).

4. That is, thirty-six instances of "for," ten of "because," seven of "as," and four of "since." In context, *et que* ("and that") functions once as *parce que* (137) and once as *comme* (190). Cf. Pierre Haffter, "L'Usage satirique des causales dans les contes de Voltaire," *Studies on Voltaire and the Eighteenth Century* 53 (1967): 7–28.

5. Jacques the Anabaptist and an officer of the Inquisition are both

shown arguing with Pangloss (146, 148), and Cunégonde *feels* that Pangloss must be wrong (154).

6. The italics are mine.

7. See Michael Danahy, "The Nature of Narrative Norms in *Candide*," *Studies on Voltaire and the Eighteenth Century* 114 (1973): 113–40.

8. Haffter, "L'Usage satirique," p.11.

9. See Danahy, "The Nature of Narrative Norms."

10. See Jean Starobinski, "*Candide* et la question de l'autorité," in Jean Macary, ed., *Essays on the Age of Enlightenment in Honor of Ira O. Wade* (Geneva: Droz, 1977), pp.305–12.

11. Apart from various prepositional phrases, participial clauses, and metalinguistic comments, we find statements supported by *c'est pour cette raison, par conséquent, en conséquence, en vertu de, voici ce qui était arrivé, la raison en était que, c'est que* ("it is for that reason," "consequently," "in consequence," "by virtue of," "here is what had happened," "the reason for it was that," "it is that"), and so on.

12. Note that the narrator can count on the narratee: they are repeatedly shown to have the same values (e.g., 155, 165, 175).

13. In other words, it should conform to something like the esthetics outlined by Pococuranté.

SIX: WRITTEN NARRATIVE

1. Gustave Flaubert, *Madame Bovary* (Paris: Gallimard and Librairie Générale Française, 1961). All page references are to this edition.

2. See, e.g., Jonathan Culler, *Flaubert: The Uses of Uncertainty* (Ithaca, N.Y.: Cornell University Press, 1974); Schor, "Pour une thématique restreinte"; and Nathaniel Wing, *The Limits of Narrative: Essays on Baudelaire, Flaubert, Rimbaud, and Mallarmé* (London: Cambridge University Press, 1986), pp.41–77.

3. For the sake of convenience, I often refer to the multiform narrative voice in the novel as "Flaubert."

4. On Larivière, see Jean-Paul Sartre, *L'Idiot de la famille*, vol. 1 (Paris: Gallimard, 1971), pp. 453–58 in particular.

5. "For every bourgeois, in the excitement of youth, has believed himself capable of immense passions, of lofty enterprises. The most mediocre libertine has dreamed of sultanas; every notary carries within him the débris of a poet" (342–43).

6. Flaubert's affection for and fascination with simpleminded or monstrous people is well known: think of Félicité in "Un Cœur simple" or of the protagonist of "La Légende de Saint-Julien l'Hospitalier."

7. Emma Bovary is, of course, not the first "Madame Bovary," and Charles's fate at the hands of Homais is that of at least three other doctors in Yonville.

8. Emma is an anti–Princesse de Clèves.

9. See Barthes, *S/Z*, pp. 145–46.

10. Schor, "Pour une thématique restreinte," argues that Homais does not speak a stilted language!

SEVEN: NARRATIVE AS ANTAGONIST

1. Guy de Maupassant, *Bel-Ami* (Paris: Garnier, 1959). All page references are to this edition.

2. Edward D. Sullivan, *Maupassant the Novelist* (Princeton, N.J.: Princeton University Press, 1954), p. 91.

3. I am referring specifically to the use of *bégayer, balbutier* ("to stammer," "to stutter") and their various forms.

4. Sullivan, *Maupassant the Novelist*, p. 92.

5. Guy de Maupassant, "Aux critiques de *Bel-Ami*—Une réponse," *Gil Blas*, June 7, 1885; reprinted in *Bel-Ami*, p. 397.

6. For an interesting view of the protagonist, see Mary Donaldson-Evans, "The Harlot's Apprentice: Maupassant's *Bel-Ami*," *French Review* 60 (1987): 616–25.

7. See 6, 271, 306, e.g. Duroy's resentment against such obvious

father figures as Forestier and Walter and his desire to supplant them are particularly noteworthy.

8. Names and their economy in *Bel-Ami* deserve to be studied. "Saint-Potin" (holy gossip), for example, is a fitting nickname. Boisrenard was "news" editor before Duroy. Madeleine constitutes the springboard propelling the protagonist toward his wedding at the church of the Madeleine. Not surprisingly, Clotilde de Marelle evokes both the game of hopscotch and the adjective or noun "mariolle" (crafty, foxy, cunning). There is also the pun on "Forestier" (275) and the fact that Jacques Rival is a duelist, that Norbert de Varenne functions like a representative of an ancient regime, and that Mme Walter's first name is, quite appropriately, Virginie.

9. Jean Alter comes to a similar conclusion in "Histoire et fiction: Les Pièges de *Bel-Ami*" (unpublished paper, n.d. [1982–85]).

10. On the question of such opponents or antimodels, see Chambers, *Story and Situation*.

11. François Tassart, *Souvenirs sur Guy de Maupassant* (Paris: Plon, 1911), pp.30–31.

12. Of course, Bel-Ami has not read Balzac (61).

13. "To tell," "teller," "tale," "story," "recite," "narrative."

14. Maupassant was from Normandy, had a reputation for sensuality, loved nature, and dreamed of money and glory. He practiced journalism himself (having some trouble, at first, and getting help from his secretary, Clémence Brun); he sometimes published the same tale in more than one newspaper; and he had *Bel-Ami* appear as a *feuilleton*. Like his protagonist, he inveighed against the hypocrisy of society, disliked obtrusive mistresses, and despised women.

15. On the subject of mirrors in *Bel-Ami*, see Sullivan, *Maupassant the Novelist*, pp.86–91; Charles Castella, "A propos de Maupassant romancier: Une Problématique des miroirs ou de la chimère du contenu historique et social," in Pierre Cogny, ed., *Le Naturalisme* (Paris: UGE,

1978), pp.361–83; and Castella, *Structures romanesques et vision sociale chez Maupassant* (Lausanne: L'Age d'Homme, 1972), pp.99–148. Like Lucien Fleurier, Georges Duroy is a being-for-others and many parallels could be developed between *Bel-Ami* and Sartre's "L'Enfance d'un chef" (cf.239–40, 307).

16. On this subject, see Castella, "A propos de Maupassant romancier," and *Structures romanesques*, as well as René Girard, *Mensonge romantique et vérité romanesque* (Paris: Grasset, 1961).

17. See, e.g., Sullivan, *Maupassant the Novelist*, p.84.

18. See André Vial, *Guy de Maupassant et l'art du roman* (Paris: Nizet, 1954).

19. Guy de Maupassant, "Les Poètes grecs contemporains," *Le Gaulois*, June 23, 1881; and "Romans," *Le Gaulois*, April 26, 1882. Quoted in Vial, *Guy de Maupassant*, pp.63, 68.

20. See Vial, *Guy de Maupassant*, p.99.

21. See Maupassant's letter to Monsieur X in *Oeuvres complètes illustrées de Guy de Maupassant*, vol.15, ed. René Dumesnil (Paris: Librairie de France, 1938), p.408.

22. Need I emphasize that the contrary obtains in many of Maupassant's tales? On the desire to tell, see Brooks, *Reading for the Plot*.

23. See Paul Bourget, *Etudes et portraits*, vol.3 (Paris: Plon, 1906), pp.30–31. See also Gerald Prince, "Architecture et thématique dans *Bel-Ami*," *Littérature*, no.71 (1988): 59–66.

24. Cf. Philippe Bonnefis, *Comme Maupassant* (Lille: Presses Universitaires de Lille, 1981), pp.27–28.

EIGHT: NAUSEA AND NARRATIVE

1. Jean-Paul Sartre, *La Nausée* (Paris: Gallimard, Collection Folio, 1938). All page references are to this edition.

2. Cf. Genette, "Vraisemblance et motivation"; and Frank Kermode, *The Sense of an Ending* (New York: Oxford University Press, 1967).

3. From this perspective, Sartre's insistence on human freedom and responsibility would be a way of narrativizing time and action, of endowing them with (a fictional) significance.

4. Roquentin is haunted by death—the coming death of Dr. Rogé (103), the possible death of M. Fasquelle (108–11), the *Mort du Célibataire* by the painter Richard Séverand (119), thoughts of killing or committing suicide—and by what in death is accidental and external to him.

5. In 1940, Sartre received the Prix du Roman Populiste for *Le Mur*!

6. On language in *La Nausée*, see Arthur C. Danto, *Jean-Paul Sartre* (New York: Viking Press, 1975), pp.1–37; Geneviève Idt, "*Les Mots*, sans les choses, sans les mots, *La Nausée*," *Degrés*, no.3 (1973): i1–i17; and Gerald Prince, "Roquentin et le langage naturel," in Michael Issacharoff and Jean-Claude Vilquin, eds., *Sartre et la mise en signe* (Lexington, Ky.: French Forum, 1982), pp.103–13.

7. See Rémy G. Saisselin, "Bouville ou l'anti-Combray," *French Review* 33 (1960): 232–38. See also Gerald Prince, *Métaphysique et technique dans l'œuvre romanesque de Sartre* (Geneva: Droz, 1968), pp.27–28.

8. The italics are mine.

9. The lyrics of "Blue Skies" are quite evocative: "Blue days, all of them gone / Nothing but blue skies / From now on . . ."

10. Balzac, *Eugénie Grandet*, p.83. On Roquentin's sexuality, see Serge Doubrovsky, "Le Neuf de cœur: Fragment d'une psycholecture de *La Nausée*," *Obliques*, nos.18–19 (1979): 67–73.

11. In *Les Mots* (Paris: Gallimard, 1964), p.54, Sartre writes: "What I have just written is false. True. Neither true nor false like everything that one writes on madmen, on men." And in *L'Idiot de la famille*, 1:39, he writes: "I confess: it's a fable. Nothing proves that it happened thus. And, worse yet, the absence of these proofs—which would necessarily be singular facts—refers us, even when we are fabulating, to schematism, to generality: my narrative fits *infants* and not Gustave in particu-

lar. No matter, I have wanted to take it to its conclusion for this one reason: the *real* explanation, I can imagine, without the least bit of vexation, that it is exactly the contrary of the one that I am inventing; *in any case*, it will have to go through the paths that I indicate and to refute mine on the site that I have defined: the body, love" (original emphasis). My reading of narrative in *La Nausée* would thus establish a continuity between the early Sartre and the later one.

12. See Denis Hollier, *Politique de la prose: Jean-Paul Sartre et l'an quarante* (Paris: Gallimard, 1982), pp.107–43 in particular. See also Gerald Prince, "Ouvertures dans *La Nausée*," *Cahiers de Sémiotique Textuelle*, 2–3 (1986): 55–65.

NINE: HOW TO REDO THINGS WITH WORDS

1. Claude Simon, *La Route des Flandres* (Paris: Editions de Minuit, 1960). All page references are to this edition.
2. See Lynn A. Higgins, "Language, the Uncanny, and the Shapes of History in Claude Simon's *The Flanders Road*," *Studies in Twentieth Century Literature* 11 (1985): 117–39.
3. Cf. Stephen Heath, *The Nouveau Roman: A Study in the Practice of Writing* (London: Elek, 1972), p.157.
4. Claude Simon, "Réponses de Claude Simon à quelques questions écrites de Ludovic Janvier," *Entretiens*, no.31 (1972): 23.
5. Claude Simon, "La Fiction mot à mot," in Jean Ricardou and Françoise van Rossum-Guyon, eds., *Nouveau Roman, hier, aujourd'hui: II Pratiques* (Paris: Union Générale d'Editions, 1972), 86–87. See also Anthony Cheal Pugh, "Describing Disaster: History, Fiction, Text and Context," in David Kelley and Isabelle Llasera, eds., *Cross-References: Modern French Theory and the Practice of Criticism* (Leeds: Society for French Studies, 1986), 112–22.
6. On language and history in *La Route des Flandres*, see David Carroll, *The Subject in Question: The Languages of Theory and the Strategies of*

Fiction (Chicago: University of Chicago Press, 1982), pp.126–39; and Higgins, "Language, the Uncanny, and the Shapes of History." I have also profited from Lucien Dällenbach, *Claude Simon* (Paris: Seuil, 1988); Heath, *The Nouveau Roman*; Salvador Jimenez-Fajardo, *Claude Simon* (Boston: Twayne, 1975), pp.54–72; J. A. E. Loubere, *The Novels of Claude Simon* (Ithaca, N.Y.: Cornell University Press, 1975), pp.86–104; and Stuart Sykes, *Les Romans de Claude Simon* (Paris: Minuit, 1979), pp.61–85.

7. In English, "how do you say," "what to call that," "what do they call that"; and "to speak the truth," "you may well say so," "I say indeed," respectively.

8. "Probably," "as if," "perhaps," "or," "or rather," "or at least," "or in any case," "so to speak," "if one may say so."

9. See Bernard Pingaud, "Sur la route des Flandres," *Les Temps Modernes*, no.178 (1961): 1026–37; Dominique Lancereaux, "Modalités de la narration dans *La Route des Flandres*," *Poétique*, no.14 (1973): 235–49; Ricardou, "Un Ordre dans la débâcle," in *Problèmes du nouveau roman*, pp.44–55; and Simon, "Réponses," pp.17, 22. See also Lucien Dällenbach, "Mise en abyme et redoublement spéculaire chez Claude Simon," in Jean Ricardou, ed., *Claude Simon* (Paris: Union Générale d'Editions, 1975), pp.151–71.

10. In fact, *c'est-à-dire* is the most frequently used repair term in the work, unless we take *comme, quelque chose comme*, and *comme si* ("like," "something like," and "as if") to constitute interchangeable repair terms. For a partial (excluding *c'est-à-dire*!) lexicological study of Simon's novel, see Janine Anseaume Kreiter, "Perception et réflexion dans *La Route des Flandres*: Signes et perception," *Romanic Review* 74 (1983): 489–94.

11. My discussion follows Michel Murat and Bernard Cartier-Bresson, "C'est-à-dire ou la reprise interprétative," *Langue Française*, no.73 (1987): 5–15. This entire number of *Langue Française*, titled "La Re-

formulation du sens dans le discours" and edited by Martin Riegel and Irene Tamba, is valuable.

12. See Madeleine Chapsal, *Quinze Ecrivains* (Paris: Julliard, 1963), p.169.

13. Maurice Merleau-Ponty, "Cinq Notes sur Claude Simon," *Médiations*, no.4 (1961–62): 5–9.

14. Of 177 occurrences of *c'est-à-dire* in *La Route des Flandres*, there are 47 in the first part, 103 in the second part, and 27 in the third part; 82 (of which 50 occur in dialogue) are tied to first-person and 95 are in third-person narration. Blum uses the term 25 times.

15. In English, my five examples would read as follows: "You can go there, that is, if you so desire"; " 'You're coming?' 'Well, I am very busy' "; "It was very cold there, that is to say, the temperature never went above 40 degrees Celsius"; "a becalmed sailboat, that is, motionless for lack of wind"; "three weeks ago, that is, a month ago."

TEN: NARRATIVE ALL THE SAME

1. Patrick Modiano, *Rue des Boutiques Obscures* (Paris: Gallimard, Collection Folio, 1978). All page references are to this edition.

2. Daniel Weissbort's English translation of the novel is titled *Missing Person* (London: Cape, 1980).

3. On the decaying grounds of Freddie's family estate, there is a "labyrinth" where Guy Roland may have played.

4. The italics are mine.

5. What does it mean for an amnesiac like Guy Roland to know that he lost his memory ten years earlier (15)?

6. To conceal the reasons for his inquiries, Guy Roland tells Stioppa de Djagoriew that he is writing a book on post-1917 Russian emigration (39).

7. "What's Left of Our Loves?," "On the Piers of Old Paris," "The Clock."

8. Also ironically, Guy Roland, who in the past may have enjoyed lead-

ing a *vie sans histoires* (212), a life without stories, without troubles, now is looking for the stories of his life.

9. The blurb emphasizes that *Rue des Boutiques Obscures* may signal "the intrusion of wandering souls in the detective novel."

10. See Alain Bony, "Suite en blanc," *Critique*, nos.469–70 (1986): 653–67; Francine de Martinoir, "Le Roman—Patrick Modiano: *Rue des Boutiques Obscures*," *Nouvelle Revue Française*, no.310 (1978): 105–8; and Marja Warehime, "Originality and Narrative Nostalgia: Shadows in Modiano's *Rue des Boutiques Obscures*," *French Forum* 12 (1987): 335–45. See also Colin W. Nettelbeck and Penelope A. Hueston, *Patrick Modiano pièces d'identité: Ecrire l'entretemps* (Paris: Lettres Modernes, 1986); and Gerald Prince, "Re-Membering Modiano, or Something Happened," *Sub-Stance*, no.49 (1986): 35–43.

Bibliography

Aarne, Antti. *Motif-Index of Folk-Literature*. Rev. and enlarged Stith Thompson. Bloomington: Indiana University Press, 1955–58.

Aarne, Antti. *The Types of the Folktale: A Classification and Bibliography*. Trans. and enlarged Stith Thompson. Helsinki: Suomolainen Tiedeakatemia, 1961.

Alleton, Viviane, Claude Bremond, and Thomas Pavel. "Vers une thématique." *Poétique*, no.64 (1985): 395–96.

Alter, Jean. "Histoire et fiction: Les Pièges de *Bel-Ami*." Unpublished paper, n.d. [1982–85].

Angenot, Marc. "Rupture et narration: Sur le 'récit dans le récit.' " *Degrés*, no.2 (1973): n1–n12.

Balzac, Honoré de. *Eugénie Grandet*. Paris: Garnier, 1965.

Barthes, Roland. *S/Z*. Paris: Seuil, 1970.

Beardsley, Monroe. *Aesthetics: Problems in the Philosophy of Criticism*. New York: Harcourt, Brace, 1958.

Bonnefis, Philippe. *Comme Maupassant*. Lille: Presses Universitaires de Lille, 1981.

Bony, Alain. "Suite en blanc." *Critique*, nos.469–70 (1986): 653–67.

Bourget, Paul. *Etudes et portraits*. Vol.3. Paris: Plon, 1906.

Bremond, Claude. "Concept et thème." *Poétique*, no.64 (1985): 415–23.

Bremond, Claude. *Logique du récit*. Paris: Seuil, 1973.

Brinker, Menachem. "Thème et interprétation." *Poétique*, no.64 (1985): 435–43.

Brooks, Peter. *Reading for the Plot: Design and Intention in Narrative*. New York: Knopf, 1984.

Calle-Gruber, Mireille. "*La Princesse de Clèves*, ou: Du refus d'être (la) fable de récits." *Degrés*, no.41 (1985): d1–d26.

Carroll, David. *The Subject in Question: The Languages of Theory and the Strategies of Fiction*. Chicago: University of Chicago Press, 1982.

Castella, Charles. "A propos de Maupassant romancier: Une Problématique des miroirs ou de la chimère du contenu historique et social." In Pierre Cogny, ed., *Le Naturalisme*, pp.361–383. Paris: UGE, 1978.

Castella, Charles. *Structures romanesques et vision sociale chez Maupassant*. Lausanne: L'Age d'Homme, 1972.

Chambers, Ross. *Meaning and Meaningfulness*. Lexington, Ky.: French Forum, 1979.

Chambers, Ross. *Story and Situation: Narrative Seduction and the Power of Fiction*. Minneapolis: University of Minnesota Press, 1984.

Chapsal, Madeleine. *Quinze Ecrivains*. Paris: Julliard, 1963.

Charles, Michel. *L'Arbre et la source*. Paris: Seuil, 1985.

Chatman, Seymour. "On the Notion of Theme in Narrative." In John Fisher, ed., *Essays in Aesthetics: Perspectives on the Work of Monroe C. Beardsley*, pp.161–79. Philadelphia: Temple University Press, 1983.

Culler, Jonathan. *Flaubert: The Uses of Uncertainty*. Ithaca, N.Y.: Cornell University Press, 1974.

Culler, Jonathan. *Structuralist Poetics: Structuralism, Linguistics, and the Study of Literature*. Ithaca: Cornell University Press, 1975.

Daemmrich, Horst S., and Ingrid Daemmrich. *Themes and Motifs in Western Literature: A Handbook*. Tübingen: Francke, 1986.

Dällenbach, Lucien. *Claude Simon*. Paris: Seuil, 1988.

Dällenbach, Lucien. "Mise en abyme et redoublement spéculaire chez Claude Simon." In Jean Ricardou, ed., *Claude Simon*, pp.151–71. Paris: Union Générale d'Editions, 1975.

Dällenbach, Lucien. *Le Récit spéculaire*. Paris: Seuil, 1977.

Danahy, Michael. "The Nature of Narrative Norms in *Candide*." *Studies on Voltaire and the Eighteenth Century* 114 (1973): 113–40.

Daneš, František. "Functional Sentence Perspective and the Organization of the Text." In František Daneš, ed., *Papers on Functional Sentence Perspective*, pp.106–28. Prague: Academic Publishing House, Czechoslovak Academy of Sciences, 1974.

Danto, Arthur C. *Jean-Paul Sartre*. New York: Viking Press, 1975.

DeJean, Joan. "Lafayette's Ellipses: The Privileges of Anonymity." PMLA 99 (1984): 884–902.

Dijk, Teun A. van. *Text and Context*. London: Longman, 1977.

Donaldson-Evans, Mary. "The Harlot's Apprentice: Maupassant's *Bel-Ami*." *French Review* 60 (1987): 616–25.

Doubrovsky, Serge. "Le Neuf de cœur: Fragment d'une psycholecture de *La Nausée*." *Obliques*, nos.18–19 (1979): 67–73.

Ducretet, Pierre R., and Marie-Paule Ducretet. *Voltaire, Candide: Etude quantitative*. Toronto: University of Toronto Press, 1974.

Ducrot, Oswald, and Tzvetan Todorov. *Dictionnaire encyclopédique des sciences du langage*. Paris: Seuil, 1972.

Falk, Eugene H. *Types of Thematic Structure*. Chicago: University of Chicago Press, 1967.

Faye, Jean-Pierre. *Le Récit hunique*. Paris: Seuil, 1967.

Flaubert, Gustave. *Madame Bovary*. Paris: Gallimard and Librairie Générale Française, 1961.

Fortescue, Michael D. *A Discourse Production Model . . . for "Twenty Questions."* Amsterdam: John Benjamins, 1980.

Frenzel, Elizabeth. *Stoff-, Motiv-, und Symbolforschung*. 4th ed. Stuttgart: Metzler, 1978.

Friedman, Norman. *Form and Meaning in Fiction*. Athens: University of Georgia Press, 1975.

Frølich, Juliette. "*La Princesse de Clèves* ou la magie du conte." *Orbis Litterarum* 34 (1979): 208–26.

Genette, Gérard. "Vraisemblance et motivation." *Communications*, no.11 (1968): 5–21.

Girard, René. *Mensonge romantique et vérité romanesque*. Paris: Grasset, 1961.

Goodman, Nelson. "About." In *Problems and Projects*, pp.246–72. Indianapolis, Ind.: Bobbs-Merrill, 1972.

Gregorio, Laurence A. *Order in the Court: History and Society in "La Princesse de Clèves."* Saratoga, Calif.: Anma Libri, 1986.

Haffter, Pierre. "L'Usage satirique des causales dans les contes de Voltaire." *Studies on Voltaire and the Eighteenth Century* 53 (1967): 7–28.

Hamon, Philippe. "Thème et effet de réel." *Poétique*, no.64 (1985): 495–503.

Heath, Stephen. *The Nouveau Roman: A Study in the Practice of Writing*. London: Elek, 1972.

Higgins, Lynn A. "Language, the Uncanny, and the Shapes of History in Claude Simon's *The Flanders Road*." *Studies in Twentieth Century Literature* 11 (1985): 117–39.

Hollier, Denis. *Politique de la prose: Jean-Paul Sartre et l'an quarante*. Paris: Gallimard, 1982.

Hutcheon, Linda. *Narcissistic Narrative: The Metafictional Paradox*. New York: Methuen, 1984.

Idt, Geneviève. "*Les Mots*, sans les choses, sans les mots, *La Nausée*." *Degrés*, no.3 (1973): i1–i17.

Jakobson, Roman. "Closing Statement: Linguistics and Poetics." In Thomas A. Sebeok, ed., *Style in Language*, pp.350–77. New York: Wiley, 1960.

Jimenez-Fajardo, Salvador. *Claude Simon*. Boston: Twayne, 1975.

Jones, Larry Bert. *Pragmatic Aspects of English Text Structure*. Dallas, Tex.: SIL Publications in Linguistics, 1983.

Jones, Linda Kay. *Theme in English Expository Discourse*. Lake Bluff, Ill.: Jupiter Press, 1977.

Judovitz, Dalia. "The Aesthetics of Implausibility: *La Princesse de Clèves*." MLN 99 (1984): 1037–56.

Kermode, Frank. *The Sense of an Ending*. New York: Oxford University Press, 1967.

Kreiter, Janine Anseaume. "Perception et réflexion dans *La Route des Flandres*: Signes et perception." *Romanic Review* 74 (1983): 489–94.

Kuizenga, Donna. *Narrative Strategies in "La Princesse de Clèves."* Lexington, Ky.: French Forum, 1976.

Labov, William. *Language in the Inner City*. Philadelphia: University of Pennsylvania Press, 1972.

La Fayette, Madame de. *La Princesse de Clèves*. Paris: Librairie Générale de France, 1958.

Lancereaux, Dominique. "Modalités de la narration dans *La Route des Flandres*." *Poétique*, no.14 (1973): 235–49.

Laugaa, Maurice. *Lectures de Mme de Lafayette*. Paris: Colin, 1971.

Li, Charles N., ed. *Subject and Topic*. New York: Academic Press, 1976.

Lotringer, Sylvère. "La Structuration romanesque." *Critique*, no.277 (1970): 498–529.

Loubere, J. A. E. *The Novels of Claude Simon*. Ithaca, N.Y.: Cornell University Press, 1975.

Lyons, John D. "Narrative, Interpretation, and Paradox: *La Princesse de Clèves*." *Romanic Review* 72 (1981): 383–400.

Martinoir, Francine de. "Le Roman—Patrick Modiano: *Rue des Boutiques Obscures*." *Nouvelle Revue Française*, no.310 (1978): 105–8.

Maupassant, Guy de. *Bel-Ami*. Paris: Garnier, 1959.

Maupassant, Guy de. *Oeuvres complètes illustrées de Guy de Maupassant*. Vol.15. Ed. René Dumesnil. Paris: Librairie de France, 1938.

Merleau-Ponty, Maurice. "Cinq Notes sur Claude Simon." *Médiations*, no.4 (1961–62): 5–9.

Miller, Nancy K. "Emphasis Added: Plots and Plausibilities in Women's Fiction." PMLA 96 (1981): 36–48.

Modiano, Patrick. *Rue des Boutiques Obscures*. Paris: Gallimard, Collection Folio, 1978.

Mortimer, Armine Kotin. "Narrative Closure and the Paradigm of Self-Knowledge in *La Princesse de Clèves*." *Style* 17 (Spring 1983): 181–95.

Moye, Richard H. "Silent Victory: Narrative, Appropriation, and Autonomy in *La Princesse de Clèves*." MLN 104 (1989): 845–60.

Murat, Michel, and Bernard Cartier-Bresson. "C'est-à-dire ou la reprise interprétative." *Langue Française*, no.73 (1987): 5–15.

Nettelbeck, Colin W., and Penelope A. Hueston. *Patrick Modiano pièces d'identité: Ecrire l'entretemps*. Paris: Lettres Modernes, 1986.

Niderst, Alain. *"La Princesse de Clèves": Le Roman paradoxal*. Paris: Larousse, 1973.

Pavel, Thomas. "Le Déploiement de l'intrigue." *Poétique*, no.64 (1985): 455–61.

Pingaud, Bernard. "Sur la route des Flandres." *Les Temps Modernes*, no.178 (1961): 1026–37.

Pratt, Mary Louise. *Toward a Speech Act Theory of Literary Discourse*. Bloomington: Indiana University Press, 1977.

Prince, Gerald. "Architecture et thématique dans *Bel-Ami*." *Littérature*, no.71 (1968): 59–66.

Prince, Gerald. *Métaphysique et technique dans l'œuvre romanesque de Sartre*. Geneva: Droz, 1968.

Prince, Gerald. *Narratology: The Form and Functioning of Narrative*. Berlin: Walter de Gruyter, 1982.

Prince, Gerald. *"Le Nœud de vipères*, ou Les destinations d'un récit." *Orbis Litterarum* 21 (1976): 72–78.

Prince, Gerald. "Ouvertures dans *La Nausée*." *Cahiers de Sémiotique Textuelle* 2–3 (1986): 55–65.

Prince, Gerald. "Récit et texte dans *Le Moyen de Parvenir*." *Neophilologus* 65 (1981): 1–5.

Prince, Gerald. "Remarques sur le *topos* et sur le dénarré." In Nicole Boursier and David Trott, eds., *La Naissance du roman en France*, pp.113–22. Paris: Biblio 17, 1990.

Prince, Gerald. "Re-Membering Modiano, or Something Happened." *Sub-Stance*, no.49 (1986): 35–43.

Prince, Gerald. "Roquentin et le langage naturel." In Michael Issacharoff and Jean-Claude Vilquin, eds., *Sartre et la mise en signe*, pp.103–13. Lexington, Ky.: French Forum, 1982.

Pugh, Anthony Cheal. "Describing Disaster: History, Fiction, Text, and Context." In David Kelley and Isabelle Llasera, eds., *Cross-References: Modern French Theory and the Practice of Criticism*, pp.112–22. Leeds: Society for French Studies, 1986.

Putnam, Hilary. "Formalization of the Concept 'About.'" *Philosophy of Science* 25 (1958): 125–30.

Reinhart, Tanya. *Pragmatics and Linguistics: An Analysis of Sentence Topics*. Bloomington: Indiana University Linguistic Club, 1982.

Ricardou, Jean. *Problèmes du nouveau roman*. Paris: Seuil, 1967.

Richard, Jean-Pierre. *Microlectures*. Paris: Seuil, 1977.

Rimmon-Kenan, Shlomith. "Qu'est-ce qu'un thème?" *Poétique*, no.64 (1985): 397–406.

Robert, Marthe. *Roman des origines et origines du roman*. Paris: Grasset, 1972.

Rousset, Jean. *Forme et signification: Essais sur les structures littéraires de Corneille à Claudel*. Paris: Corti, 1962.

Ryan, Marie-Laure. "Embedded Narratives and Tellability." *Style* 20 (1986): 319–40.

Saisselin, Rémy G. "Bouville ou l'anti-Combray." *French Review* 33 (1960): 232–38.

Sareil, Jean. "La Description négative." *Romanic Review* 78 (1987): 1–9.

Sareil, Jean. *Essai sur Candide*. Geneva: Droz, 1967.

Sartre, Jean-Paul. *L'Idiot de la famille*. Vol. 1. Paris: Gallimard, 1971.

Sartre, Jean-Paul. *Les Mots*. Paris: Gallimard, 1964.

Sartre, Jean-Paul. *La Nausée*. Paris: Gallimard, Collection Folio, 1938.

Schor, Naomi. "Pour une thématique restreinte: Ecriture, parole, et différence dans Madame Bovary." *Littérature*, no.22 (1976): 30–46.

Shklovsky, Victor. "Art and Technique." In Lee T. Lemon and Marion J. Reis, eds., *Russian Formalist Criticism*, pp.3–24. Lincoln: University of Nebraska Press, 1965.

Simon, Claude. "La Fiction mot à mot." In Jean Ricardou and Françoise van Rossum-Guyon, eds., *Nouveau Roman: Hier, aujourd'hui: II Pratiques*, pp.73–97. Paris: Union Générale d'Editions, 1972.

Simon, Claude. "Réponses de Claude Simon à quelques questions écrites de Ludovic Janvier." *Entretiens*, no.31 (1972): 15–29.

Simon, Claude. *La Route des Flandres*. Paris: Editions de Minuit, 1960.

Sperber, Dan, and Deirdre Wilson. *Relevance: Communication and Cognition*. Oxford: Basil Blackwell, 1986.

Starobinski, Jean. "*Candide* et la question de l'autorité." In Jean Macary, ed., *Essays on the Age of Enlightenment in Honor of Ira O. Wade*, pp.305–12. Geneva: Droz, 1977.

Strawson, P. F. "Identifying References and Truth Values." *Theoria* 30 (1964): 96–118.

Sullivan, Edward D. *Maupassant the Novelist*. Princeton, N.J.: Princeton University Press, 1954.

Sykes, Stuart. *Les Romans de Claude Simon*. Paris: Minuit, 1979.

Tassart, François. *Souvenirs sur Guy de Maupassant*. Paris: Plon, 1911.

Todorov, Tzvetan. *Poétique de la prose (choix): Suivi de nouvelles recherches sur le récit*. Paris: Seuil, 1978.

Trousson, Raymond. *Le Thème de Prométhée dans la littérature européenne*. 2 vols. Geneva: Droz, 1964.

Verrier, Jean. "Le Récit réfléchi." *Littérature*, no. 5 (1972): 58–68.

Vial, André. *Guy de Maupassant et l'art du roman*. Paris: Nizet, 1954.

Voltaire. *Candide, ou l'Optimisme*. In *Romans et Contes*. Paris: Garnier, 1960.

Warehime, Marja. "Originality and Nostalgia: Shadows in Modiano's *Rue des Boutiques Obscures*." *French Forum* 12 (1987): 335–45.

Wilson, Deirdre, and Dan Sperber. "On Grice's Theory of Conversation." In Paul Werth, ed., *Conversation and Discourse: Structure and Interpretation*, pp. 155–78. New York: St. Martin's Press, 1981.

Wimmers, Inge Crosman. *Poetics of Reading: Approaches to the Novel*. Princeton, N.J.: Princeton University Press, 1988.

Wing, Nathaniel. *The Limits of Narrative: Essays on Baudelaire, Flaubert, Rimbaud, and Mallarmé*. London: Cambridge University Press, 1986.

Zholkovsky, Alexander. *Themes and Texts: Toward a Poetics of Expressiveness*. Ithaca, N.Y.: Cornell University Press, 1984.

Index

Aarne, Antti, 16, 20; *Motif Index of Folk Literature*, 16; *The Types of the Folktale*, 16
Angenot, Marc, 22
A Thousand and One Nights, 18, 25-26, 74
Autothematizing, 15, 17

Balzac, Honoré de, 11, 12, 18, 69, 97, 101; *Eugénie Grandet*, vii, 8-13, 97, 98, 101; *Sarrasine*, 18, 26
Barrès, Maurice, 97
Barthes, Roland, 15, 17, 18
Beckett, Samuel, 30
Benjamin, Walter, 15
Benoit, Pierre, 97
Beroalde de Verville, 16; *Le Moyen de Parvenir*, 16
Blanchot, Maurice, 15; *Le Livre à venir*, 15
Bordeaux, Henry, 97
Bourget, Paul, 97
Bremond, Claude, 15, 31, 36
Brooks, Peter, 18

Camus, Albert, ix; *La Peste*, ix, 26, 38
Céline, Louis-Ferdinand, 15, 119; *Voyage au bout de la nuit*, 15
Cervantes, Miguel de: *Don Quijote*, 17, 18
Charles, Michel, 14
Chaucer, Geoffrey, 29; *Troilus and Criseyde*, 29
Culler, Jonathan, 28

Dickens, Charles: *Bleak House*, 1
Dijk, Teun A. van, 2
Disnarrated, viii, ix, 28-38, 40, 111
Dostoevsky, Fyodor, 23
Dumas, Alexandre, 87

Faye, Jean-Pierre, 18
Fernandez, Ramon, 15
Flaubert, Gustave, 4, 65, 66, 67, 70-75; "Un Cœur simple," 4; *Madame Bovary*, viii, 38, 65-76
Frame, 2, 5, 7, 9-13, 21. *See also* Thematic frame

Friedman, Norman, 1; *Form and Meaning in Fiction*, 1
Frye, Northrop, 1

Gautier, Théophile, 29; *Mademoiselle de Maupin*, 29
Gide, André: *L'Immoraliste*, 26; *La Porte étroite*, 26
Goodman, Nelson, 3
Good narrative, viii, 38, 63-64, 67, 72, 73, 75, 76, 79

Haffter, Pierre, 55
Hamon, Philippe, 20
Hemingway, Ernest: *A Farewell to Arms*, 1
History, 16, 91, 95, 103, 108-11
Homer, *The Odyssey*, 18
Hugo, Victor, 69

Kafka, Franz, 25; *The Castle*, 25
Kristeva, Julia, 20

Labov, William, 31, 36
La Fayette, Madame de, 29, 39, 40, 46, 49; *La Princesse de Clèves*, viii, 29, 38, 39-50
La Fontaine, Jean de, 16; "La Jeune Veuve," 16, 26; "Le Lion et le chasseur," 16; "Le Pouvoir des fables," 16
Lancereaux, Dominique, 114
La Queste del Saint Graal, 16, 18
Lyotard, Jean-François, 96

Marguerite de Navarre, 41

Maupassant, Guy de, 77, 78, 80-82, 84, 86-90; Bel-Ami, viii, 77-90
Mauriac, François: *Le Nœud de vipères*, 16, 26
Memory, 73, 74, 83, 106, 124-26, 128, 129
Merleau-Ponty, Maurice, 116
Modiano, Patrick, 121; *Rue des Boutiques Obscures*, viii, 121-32
Motif, 1-5, 13, 16

Narratability. *See* Tellability
Narratable, 18
Narrative, vii-ix, 13, 15-19, 21, 22, 24, 26, 31, 34, 36, 39, 42, 45, 94-95, 106, 108, 131-32; and life, viii, 94-95; as theme, vii-ix, 14-27, 38; and truth, vii-ix, 27, 38, 50. *See also* Good narrative
Narrativity, viii, 28, 36
Narratology, 15, 18, 19
Nonnarratable. *See* Unnarratable
Nonnarrated. *See* Unnarrated

Pavel, Thomas, 20
Perrault, Charles, 4; "Le Petit Chaperon rouge," 4
Pingaud, Bernard, 114
Plausibility, 45-50, 93
Plot, 2, 3-5, 18
Pratt, Mary Louise, 31
Proust, Marcel: *A la recherche du temps perdu*, 38, 99
Putnam, Hilary, 3

Reinhart, Tanya, 3
Ricardou, Jean, 16, 114
Rousseau, Jean-Jacques, 87, 108
Ryan, Marie-Laure, 31, 36

Sand, Georges, 69, 87
Sareil, Jean, 52
Sartre, Jean-Paul, 15, 25, 91, 99; *La Nausée*, viii, 15, 25, 91-103
Saussure, Ferdinand de, 20
Schor, Naomi, 13, 74
Scudéry, Mlle de, 87
Sénard, Marie-Antoine-Jules, 71
Shklovsky, Victor, 31; "Art and Technique," 31
Simon, Claude, 104, 106, 109-11, 113-17, 119; *La Route des Flandres*, viii, 104-20
Soulié, Frédéric, 87
Sterne, Laurence, *Tristram Shandy*, 16
Strawson, P. F., 3
Subject. *See* Topic
Sue, Eugène, 87
Sullivan, Edward D., 77, 78; *Maupassant the Novelist*, 77
Symbol, 4, 5, 13

Tassart, François, 81

Tellability, 28, 30, 39
Thematic designation, 38
Thematic focalization, 38
Thematic frame, 7, 9, 16, 17, 19
Thematic relief, 24, 27, 38
Thematics, vii, 13, 15, 21-23
Theme, vii, 1-13, 14, 19, 20-25, 37, 38
Theme of narrative. *See* Narrative: as theme
Themer, 6, 8, 9, 11, 13, 18, 20
Theming, vii, 3, 6-8, 13, 19, 21-22, 25-26
Thompson, Stith, 16, 20. *See also* Aarne, Antti
Todorov, Tzvetan, 16, 18
Tolstoy, Leo: *War and Peace*, 17
Topic, 2-5, 13
Topos, 4, 13, 37

Unnarratable, 28-30, 34
Unnarrated, 30, 34

Voltaire, 52; *Candide*, viii, ix, 26, 38, 51-64
Vraisemblable. See Plausibility

Zholkovsky, Alexander, 21-22, 24

LIBRARY